Praise for Education: A for Change

'Richard Gerver's book gives a personal yet authoritative account of the current state of UK education, and also provides a refreshingly optimistic perspective on where we might go next.'

Geoff Barton, General Secretary, Association of School and College Leaders, @RealGeoffBarton

'Richard Gerver not only writes about optimism, he exemplifies it and we desperately need that now. It is an optimism founded in his wide and unique experience and definitely worth sharing. Read this book!'

David Cameron, Education Consultant, @realdcameron

'In this refreshing, honest and deeply personal book, Richard Gerver builds on all his international experience to set out a manifesto for change in education, with collaboration, openness and optimism at its core.'

Steve Munby, Visiting Professor at UCL London Institute of Education, @steve_munby

'In this powerful book, Gerver calls for a collaborative vision for education that will prepare society to "thrive in uncertainty". He shares sharp insight, achieved through school leadership, uniquely combined with global experience of working with eminent leaders throughout industry. A great read.'

Dame Alison Peacock, Chief Executive, Chartered College of Teaching, @AlisonMPeacock

'Intelligent, passionate, honest and at times contentious, Richard Gerver does not simply present a manifesto for education. He gives us joined-up thinking about how education, business and society can work and succeed together.'

Steve Wheeler, Author and Speaker, @SteveWheeler

Other titles from Bloomsbury Education

Creating Tomorrow's Schools Today by Richard Gerver

Ten Traits of Resilience: Achieving positivity and purpose in school leadership by James Hilton

Leading from the Edge: A school leader's guide to recognising and overcoming stress by James Hilton

Narrowing the Attainment Gap: A handbook for schools by Daniel Sobel

Leading on Pastoral Care by Daniel Sobel

Achievement for All: Raising aspirations, access and achievement by Sonia Blandford and Catherine Knowles

Education:
A Manifesto
for Change

A personal reflection on
the future of education

Richard Gerver

Foreword by Ross Morrison McGill

BLOOMSBURY EDUCATION

LONDON   OXFORD   NEW YORK   NEW DELHI   SYDNEY

BLOOMSBURY EDUCATION
Bloomsbury Publishing Plc
50 Bedford Square, London, WC1B 3DP, UK

BLOOMSBURY, BLOOMSBURY EDUCATION and the Diana logo are trademarks of
Bloomsbury Publishing Plc

First published in Great Britain 2019

A catalogue record for this book is available from the British Library

ISBN: PB: 978-1-4729-6236-2; ePDF: 978-1-4729-6237-9; ePub: 978-1-4729-6238-6

2 4 6 8 10 9 7 5 3 1 (paperback)

Typeset by Newgen KnowledgeWorks Pvt. Ltd., Chennai, India
Printed and bound in Great Britain by CPI Group (UK) Ltd, Croydon CR0 4YY

To find out more about our authors and books visit www.bloomsbury.com
and sign up for our newsletters

To Stamps…

You gave me so many of the tools for my future…

RIP x

Contents

Acknowledgements

I started my journey as an adult, prepared for the challenges of my future thanks to my family and certain teachers of my own; I name you in this book.

My career as a teacher is down to my amazing wife Lynne and my training at the University of Derby.

The best years of my professional life and of my own learning were spent in the three schools in which I was privileged enough to work: Chaddesden Park Junior, St John's CE Primary and, of course, Grange; to all of the staff, pupils and wider communities who welcomed me, nurtured me and ultimately trusted me, thank you all!

To the guiding lights who have influenced, encouraged and constructively criticised my thoughts, actions and words as an educator: Sir Ken Robinson, James Hilton, Pam Earlam, Les Seymour, et al. I hope that I am a part of your legacies.

To Hannah Marston and the team at Bloomsbury, thank you so much for letting me share my passion one more time.

Finally, to all of you who commit your energy, passion, professionalism and purpose to working with our children every single day, in order to help them to live fulfilling and meaningful lives… words are not enough but because of you, the world could be so bright!

Foreword

Richard Gerver has over 25 years' experience of working in schools and more recently education settings across the world. He is someone we should listen to and, as an educator, he has continued to inspire me over the past five years, ever since I first read his work and invited him in to present a keynote at one of my schools.

There reaches a point in every teacher's career when they have to walk away from a job they love. This has been a decision that both Richard and I have taken in the past decade and, as Richard describes, it is one of those 'lump-in-throat' moments.

In this heartwarming book, Richard reminds the reader of the footprints teachers and school leaders have every day: they make thousands and thousands of idiosyncratic decisions in the classroom, which, at a whole-school level, make a collective difference to the lives of children. Those working in our schools will be familiar with political rhetoric versus our legacy; the reality that our internal decisions have little or no value for metrics and accountability, but define a teacher's impact on developing a child's love of learning. This sociological data, which is hard to quantify, is given no value when it comes to school improvement.

A key sentence in Richard's introduction is this line from a colleague listening to him speak at an event: 'I never thought I'd get the chance to hear you speak, as I'd been told that you were no longer involved in education.' Here Richard explains why he has retreated from the front-line educational debate, unpicking the truth behind the challenges of working for oneself, as well as explaining why his perspective on education has changed. As I find myself also sitting on the other side of the fence, I can understand why this perspective is offered, but stepping into a world that Richard has now embraced for ten years, I believe I have never been more immersed in education at a whole-system level than I am now. Although physically I may not be attached to one school, like Richard, I find myself working in schools every week or speaking with fellow educators on a daily basis all across the world. This perspective has given Richard a wider lens to remind us, and share his insights about, why we need change from the ground up.

Richard discusses what he has learnt from his travels about assessment, curriculum and socio-economic issues, highlighting what, why and how other countries are moving towards more efficient systems, with less focus on testing, and towards new models that can better develop young people as well as educational institutions. As Richard articulates with passion and simplicity, our education model is reactive rather than proactive and in the final chapter of the book, he shares a fascinating alternative to lessen academic burdens.

As an active user of social media, I can see a clear division between various educators online. Views are often shared that are underpinned by political bias, positioning or philosophical interests and are designed to undermine, as Richard writes, 'constructive discussions and observations' about how best to meet the needs of our children. Richard explains that education is at its worst when it is adversarial and, as one of the most active educators on social media in the UK, I know this debate is often exposed and heightened through transparent, or sometimes vitriolic and hidden, networks. In truth, although I hope to unpick some of this evidence and influence in the doctoral research I am currently conducting at the University of Cambridge, Richard shows why there has rarely been any potential for social media to help us find a new way forward. Whether social media helps us to achieve a manifesto for change or not, collaboration, a shared purpose and a clear vision for all stakeholders in education must be our future.

Name-calling, polarisation and a lack of teamwork do nothing to help a child to make progress in school, and if some educators of influence continue to behave in this way, do we genuinely believe we can achieve a balanced solution? Richard explains how in some of the schools and organisations he has visited, culture feeds success, and he explores why trust has been sucked out of our schools to be replaced with high-stakes accountability at a micro level.

A common purpose that makes a profound difference to the lives of children and supports the moral compass of our educators can be found in successful businesses, schools and organisations. Countries such as South Korea and Finland regularly make the media headlines but jurisdictions such as Israel are also renowned for constructing their education systems sociologically to instil a common goal for their people. We can learn a great deal from looking overseas, but we also need to look more closely within our own system to find the answers we so desperately need.

If we are to achieve any certainty, we need trust, knowledge and common goals. Richard highlights some interesting examples of each from a wide range of organisations. He explains how collaboration and bringing people together informally, in a shared space, often without an agenda, is so powerful. This is quite the opposite of what we see in most of our educational settings, where we construct groups of children by age or subject – far from the reality of what *actually* happens day-to-day in the real world and how people live and work.

Of course, the answer isn't simple and to make a real change will require people from all sectors of the education community coming together to think deeply about the purpose of education not only to discuss but also to rethink how we can meet the needs of our children to ensure parents, politicians and most of all teachers have answered one of the simplest yet most complex questions about education: what is the purpose of school?

Richard reminds us that we must be prepared to leave our comfort zones and put aside our bias and egos if we genuinely want a better society. He highlights what I have observed over the past ten years on social media: that there are people within the system who are happy to promote fragmentation and a blurring of purpose and polarisation. To prevent this dichotomy from evolving further in our society, we must reclaim our voices so that every child is included. How we do this, Richards suggests, is to go 'beyond the walls' of our own perspective.

Once a teacher, always a teacher. This is true, but it does not mean that this is all that a teacher can do. 'I'm just a teacher': for years I have said this myself and have heard it on the lips of thousands of other teachers, particularly when introducing themselves to others in a formal setting. Teachers are humble beings who do not know their true potential and, with high-stakes accountability, teachers are under significant pressure and rarely have the time to seek innovation.

Research published by The Varkey Foundation in November 2018 (Dolton et al., 2018) highlighted that 'teachers' perceptions of themselves' are actually lower than public perceptions of teachers. The study from 35 countries highlights that we, therefore, should become more confident in our capabilities. As a school leader, I started to develop a wide range of experience and expertise, and as I stepped nervously out of the classroom for the very first time in 25 years, little did I realise how deep and complex my skill set had become, from having the ability to speak on a stage in front of 500 people, to running a business and having my views shared with educators around the world. When I left school in 2017, little did I know that two years later I would be influencing national policy, conducting groundbreaking research and travelling the world to work with schools.

Teachers are a rare breed: intelligent, articulate and experts in people and their behaviours. There are not many other professions that know the human being better – what drives them and how to seek improvement. If teachers could mobilise themselves, they would be able to shape policy. So, imagine what we could all do if we got ourselves organised. Richard strikes a chord in all of us when he reminds us of how we have developed as a human race. Society has not evolved simply because of a focus on efficiency, but because of our curiosity and desire to learn. This book manifests itself in many forms. It is not a how-to practical guidebook for teachers but rather a heads-up and 'take a look around you' read for those who want to understand what is happening in education and how we may solve it, together, with optimism.

There is no single way to improve schools, no structure or label, but there are people, and it is the workforce who can take on the challenge of school improvement. If we can reach the moon, cultivate an embryo and grow a human ear on the back of a mouse, then we can certainly design schools that are fit for purpose to support children's mental health, reduce exclusions and allow all of our children to leave with a set of qualifications so that they can contribute to wider society.

What I hope you take away from Richard's book is not just a soundbite from the title, but an understanding of how you can use your experiences within education to collectively produce change. How you do this relies entirely on your knowledge of teaching, your experiences and, most of all, your capacity and desire to make a switch, but if I could add one piece of advice to this brilliant book, it would be a call to arms to recognise your passion. Find your niche and gather people around you who can give you the belief that change *can* happen. Tomorrow, rather than end a conversation with your critics with a 'Yes, but…', start a conversation with a 'Yes, and…', and ask how you can both work together to solve the issues we face.

Our schools can only be as good as the people who want to improve them. It starts with you, and it needs to start now.

Ross Morrison McGill, January 2019

Ross Morrison McGill also known as @TeacherToolkit, the 'most followed educator on social media in the UK', is the founder of one of the most popular education websites in the world. He is an award-winning blogger, author and teacher with 26 years' experience of working in schools. The Sunday Times *listed him as one of the '500 most influential people in Britain'. Ross remains the only classroom teacher to have featured to this day.*

Introduction

I left the front line of education in 2007 after a 16-year career as a teacher and headteacher. To this day, the decision to leave remains the most difficult and emotional moment of my professional life.

I eventually chose a career in education after a few years of trying to find my direction, aspiration and sense of value after leaving school myself in 1987. It was a tough but extraordinary time for me. I had done okay at school; I was average, academically and sportingly. If I had a talent, it lay in the arts but I was no game changer.

After 15 years of formal education, I walked out of the gates of my school with my friends and peers for the last time in June 1987; many were off to university, some to jobs, and me? Well, as I walked out for that last time, I was heading out to be something, I thought, but I had no idea what.

Over the next couple of years I did a little acting, tried advertising sales, estate agency, copywriting and even sold the very first 'mobile phones'. Eventually I decided to head back into higher education.

It was during that first happy year, a year when, for the first time in my life, I experienced the joy of being surrounded by likeminded people all studying something we loved, something we all related to and felt mattered to us, that a passion for learning was reignited in me for the first time since I was 13 or 14 years old.

My decision to teach was crystallised during that first joyous year at college. As I look back on it, thanks for that epiphany were due to three people.

Firstly, my mother, a woman who had not only given everything to raise my brother and me but a woman who had had the courage to allow us to follow our own dreams, passions and pathways, even if, for the most part, they resulted in dead ends. She bestowed in me a belief that I would find a passion and, when I did, I'd know it and that I would then go at it hard, with commitment, enthusiasm and desire.

Secondly, there was a fellow student, a young woman, training to be a teacher, who, having agreed to a first date, gave me the chance to understand a little about education from a teacher's eye. She was a practical, organised and determined person, who taught me so many of the disciplines I lacked. It was she who encouraged me to believe I could teach and that I should go on from my degree and complete a teaching qualification. Nearly 30 years on she is still my driver and has transmitted the same qualities on to our own children.

Finally, there was David: MY teacher. We all have one. He taught me English and drama from the time I was nine until I went to secondary school. When I first started thinking about becoming a teacher, it was the memory of him – the person, the educator, the inspiration, the life changer – that flashed into my mind's eye and confirmed my desire to make a real difference to the next generation.

When I eventually began my teaching career and throughout it, I obsessed over one question: what did I want the students I was lucky enough to teach to look like as human beings when they left my care? It's a question I have asked many times. I am sure that I am not the only person to have chosen to become a teacher for what some may say were ideological reasons, but they were crucial drivers for me and remain so to this day.

I wanted to become a teacher to help to prepare others to live their own lives happily, with purpose and with success. At my most ideological, I wanted to help to prepare future generations to lead the world to even better places, to find solutions to issues around the environment, the economy, equity and social cohesion that have come to dominate our age.

Selfishly, I wanted to make a difference.

I will never forget my last day as an educator, saying goodbye to colleagues and children for that final time: people who had become a family. In that final job, as Headteacher of Grange Primary School, our shared experience of creating something remarkable was the hardest thing to walk away from.

Recently, a happy series of coincidences led me to meet up with some of the teachers from my very first teaching job. They are long retired now and I was invited to speak at their annual retired teachers' lunch. It was a deeply moving experience, sharing their memories of the various children and events that still lived with them today. Some, now quite old, spoke with passion for the jobs they once did; the light in their eyes ignited when they talked about Lucy, Tom or Ashraf; their pride in knowing that they had made a difference.

Only days later, I had a reunion with some of the staff from Grange and of course, as old colleagues do, we talked about some of our former students; strikingly, many have gone on to become teachers themselves – lump-in-throat time for sure.

I found myself reminiscing about my own career.

In 2010, my first book, *Creating Tomorrow's Schools Today*, was published. I had never intended to write a book and actually, in its first draft, it was just a personal reflection on my teaching career, my beliefs and my experiences at Grange. It will always be that for me but I was lucky as it captured the interest of educators and parents worldwide and, by so doing, opened up a whole new world for me. A world that has taken me not only on geographical adventures but cultural ones too; it has also given me the chance to meet and experience lives and environments well beyond education. It has led to me being given access to world leaders, sporting icons, cultural heroes and business titans. I would be lying if I told you it hadn't been amazing – a recent life filled with pinch-yourself moments.

Towards the end of 2017, however, I was giving a speech in Edinburgh about education and its future. After my input, a young teacher came up to me and asked me to sign a well-thumbed copy of *Creating Tomorrow's Schools Today*. She smiled, thanked me and then said, 'I never thought I'd get the chance to hear you speak, as I'd been told that you were no longer involved in education.' I was a little taken aback but understood what she was saying.

That was the final straw and the catalyst for this book.

The truth is that once a teacher, always a teacher. You just have to spend time with the retired teachers from previous generations and iterations of education to understand that. When I left Grange and the front line, I never saw it as walking away from teaching. It wasn't because I'd become disillusioned or bored; it was because I truly believed that I had the opportunity, at that time, to broaden my own knowledge, experience and education. I had also been reminded by my wife that I had spent my career urging my students to seize opportunity and to have the courage to take risks in order to realise their potential, and that I should do the same.

Whilst I hadn't planned to write another book about education, a number of key experiences over the last ten years have increasingly meant that I knew I had thoughts and ideas I needed to share.

In the decade since I left Grange, I have travelled to and worked in some of the most interesting and dynamic education systems in the world: Finland, South Korea, Singapore, Hong Kong, China and Colombia. I have even had the honour of working with schools in Pakistan. What is clear is that they are all focused on the future, not the past, and are all researching new models of learning that will best prepare their young people for that future. As a result, they are asking crucial questions about testing, curriculum, socio-economics and health. Many, including China and Singapore, have made the brave decision to move away from focusing on making their systems more efficient and test-focused, in order to find new models and pathways that better develop young people for a future that can no longer be about seeking out and locking down certainty, but a world that is exponentially changing and challenging: a world that is filled with both increasing opportunity and challenge. In the book, I will cite examples of this and how it should influence our own thinking and practice.

During my travels I have also had the chance to meet, talk to and work with people who have helped to shape the world we are living in and transitioning to: people such as Apple co-founder Steve Wozniak, who believes that we spend too long talking about what we should teach and not enough about how people should learn, a belief underlined by the philosophy that he and Steve Jobs actioned when recruiting in the early days at Apple by 'never employing anyone who needed man-aging'. This is something that his first employer, Nolan Bushnell, the founder of

Atari, underlined when talking to me about the future of work and the need for a higher value of human skills that will be at an increasing premium, with the advent of artificial intelligence (AI) and other disruptive technologies.

These provocations are further supported by globally significant reports on the future of education, skills and work, such as the 2013 'Skills Outlook' produced by the Organisation for Economic Co-operation and Development (OECD). This report cites four key challenges for us to consider as we develop policy on the future of education in order to ensure that young people are to be most effectively prepared for the future:

1. To review the over-reliance and focus on formal qualifications rather than the development of actual skills.
2. To ensure the understanding of the importance of interpersonal skills over routine cognition.
3. To understand the increasing importance of people learning to adapt and change.
4. To explore closer links between the worlds of work and education.

These findings were further underlined to me by a man whom I regard as a personal hero, the former President of the United States of America, Barack Obama, who told me when we met in the summer of 2018 that the current models of education prevalent in countries like the US and the UK need far greater thought. He believes that the model created to take people from farms to factories and offices, a model that focused almost entirely on academic and technical development, needs radical evolution if we are to help young people in the pursuit of a different future in a different world.

Amongst all of the chaos, confusion and uncertainty in the modern world, I have come to believe that we are on the verge of a new renaissance, a deeply human one that will be led by our children. I want to explore how we can best support them through their education to aid that possibility.

As educators we must be people passionate about the future and the people who can create it: our children. We must always find the strength and energy to consider our legacy and not to be engulfed by the stress and pressure of the right now. This book will articulate my own personal vision for that legacy, which is essentially built around the gravitational pull of how we help the next generation to be:

- healthy
- skilled
- aware
- hopeful
- of value.

I worry that on a policy and headline level, education is still stuck in a reactive mode, one still striving for efficiency rather than change, desperate to rediscover some long-lost sense of certainty – of a world where we felt safe and secure, a world that I am afraid no longer exists. That is no reason to mourn, however, or to feel worried. The future is, as it always has been, bright; yes, there are and will be challenges, some grave, but we are a remarkable species who can always do better and be better. Education, great education, can be a significant steer for that, if we take the time and find the courage to embrace it.

As a result, as an educator, I have never been more passionate about education and about what we all need to do, together, to ensure we give young people the very best platform in life to aspire and achieve, to dream and then to turn those dreams into reality, to have hope that leads to ambition, purpose and a profound sense of value.

I have deliberately withdrawn from the front-line educational debate over the last few years; that is a truth and in the first chapter I'll explain why but I don't believe that education has ever been more important than it is now. This book is not a how-to guide; there are far better qualified people than me, producing stunning, practical advice for teachers. This book is not meant to be a heads-down, professional manual. I want this book to be a heads-up, big-picture piece, one that I urge you to use to debate, discuss and develop new visions and values, whether you are an educator, a parent, a carer or someone with an interest in education, who wants to get involved.

My aim is to share my experiences and thoughts about education since leaving the chalkface. It is an exploration of the world as I have seen it and what I believe that means for us all and, most pertinently, for our children as we continue to head into the unknown. It is, in essence, a response to my primary reflex of so much of what I have encountered over the last ten years.

I wish I knew then what I know now.

1
Peace!

'Former adversaries can come together to find common ground in a way that benefits all their people, to let go of the past and embrace the future, to forgive and to reconcile.'

William Jefferson Clinton (2000)

When I reflect on my career in education I can think of many ups and many downs; I also remember great periods of frustration and anger. I am as guilty as any for some of the things I've said and done in the heat of the education debate.

Some years ago, I met an incredible educator: passionate, committed and brave. She comes from the polar opposite view to me politically and philosophically. She is eloquent, highly intelligent and driven. If I'm honest, I was intimidated by her. My reaction to meeting her still haunts me to this day.

After two hours of conversation and debate we hugged; it was genuine because despite our obvious differences, what was clear to us both was our common ground; we both did what we did because we both cared passionately about children, about education and about its ability to make a real difference to all kids, everywhere. We had discovered a mutuality that I believe could have led to a real opportunity for collaboration and shared understanding. A few days later, I was delivering a keynote at a teachers' conference and I made a cheap jibe at this educator's expense. Even as I write now, I feel shame. Tragically, I had tainted the relationship before it had begun. I had betrayed her trust and for that I will always feel a profound regret, but the greatest damage I did that day was to ruin the potential to stand on common ground and find a new way forward for education, together.

I am well aware that education goes in cycles; it ebbs and flows dependent on the politics, policies and government of the day but what saddens me most is when it becomes adversarial.

In 2007 when I left my headship, we were in a period of relative calm. There was mature debate around the future of education. These things are all relative, but there was a sense of collaboration, of shared purpose and vision, but by the time my first book was published in 2010, things had changed. The vitriol, name-calling and accusatory nature around the future of schooling had returned and with a vengeance. Great teachers are, by their very nature, socially aware and, by their instincts, healers; they want to make a positive difference and that's the reason why it hurts me to see so many spending so long at each other's throats. I am not naive enough to believe that education can ever be divorced from politics but it is never good when politics uses education as a weapon. As Abraham Maslow (1966) said, 'If the only tool you have is a hammer, you tend to see every problem as a nail.'

The problem in essence is that as we get sucked into the whirlpool, we spend so much of our time and energy focused on constructing division and trying to disprove and discredit others that we take our eyes off what really matters: our children, their future and what education can do to constructively make a difference. We are living in a time where polarisation, hatred and division are almost the norm: a world where some express their own anxieties and uncertainties by attacking others; it seems that the reptilian part of our brain is in the ascendant. As educators we have always had a responsibility to be role models, to endeavour to reflect the best of society, and that has never been more important than it is today. In this chapter, I want to explore both the challenges we face around anger and hate as a society and how, as teachers, we can do something about this by modelling the fact that we really do have more in common than that which divides us.

Social media: a catalyst of division?

The advent of social media has been both a blessing and a curse, both in the education world and in much wider contexts. Used responsibly and maturely, it is a fantastic tool for collaboration, support and engagement. On Twitter, for example, users such as @TeacherToolkit in the education sphere have proved that. The danger, however, is that it is also an ecosystem for hate and for constructing confrontation in order to get noticed and to generate division. Social media also gives people a space in which they can vent their frustrations and concerns in public whilst maintaining anonymity. Some of what is said and stated cannot be held to account and at times can lead to a kind of Wild-West style, lynch-mob mentality.

I made the choice, a few years ago, to largely withdraw from the education debate on social media for that reason. I began to notice a worrying shift away from the mature, objective learning tool that was developing, especially in places like Scandinavia, to one that was being hijacked by people who wanted to undermine and personalise constructive discussions and observations.

In many ways, some of the polarisation in education has only reflected the hatred and anger that have become themes of the 21st century, maybe catalysed by the global financial crisis in 2007/08 and then stoked by social media. Let's hope that they don't become the historic legacy of the century. Let's hope that we can model and help our children to understand better the challenges around social media.

To recognise how we can change course, we perhaps need to explore some of that wider context. 2016 was a year that truly highlighted both the power and the danger of social media and its use to harvest and focus hatred and division in world-changing contexts. Irrespective of whether you were pro or anti events such as Brexit or even pro or anti the extraordinary election of President Donald J. Trump, the social impact of both have been seismic but have not led to anything other than further polarisation and anger. In the interests of honesty, first let me say this: I was both pro-Europe and anti-Trump but I want to explore both as objectively as I can. Both historic events served to underline to me the angry age in which we live and, for the record, I do not accept or countenance the view that people who didn't agree with me on the issues that led to the events highlighted were crazy, naive or even stupid. Even when I look at events around Europe and the world that have led to a resurgence of racial and social extremism, fascism, fundamentalism and intolerance, I don't blame many, despite the fact that I personally find it abhorrent. I guess that my instinct as a teacher is to work out why and ask of myself what I can do to make a difference.

To an extent, how we move forward from here and, in particular, how we use education to redirect ourselves and our children will define that. I think we, as educators, can help to solve this increasing sense of divide and this growing bitterness. Looking back on the events of 2016 and how they relate to the 2007 crisis, I think that there is much for us to learn and to think about. I believe that the ten intervening years should stand as a watershed moment for education.

In pursuit of certainty

In essence, mass education has in part been designed around training our children to seek out certainty – to help them understand what direction their academic abilities could take them and then to encourage them to get their heads down and do everything in their power to prepare for that, in order to create a clear path, a narrative for their lives. Be it lawyer, doctor, construction worker, dancer, beautician, engineer or software designer, the socially responsible view was to help kids lock it down and then achieve it, so that they could own a home, contribute to the economy, the state and their own financial security – all worthy and vital for a functioning society.

The flaw, though, is that as the century has progressed, certainty has become increasingly elusive. Globalisation, technological advancement and environment shifts, for example, have changed the game, and that was accelerated, not caused by, the global collapse in 2007.

There is no greater cause of stress than insecurity or a perception of a lack of control over the events in one's life. We are simply not educated to exist happily in that kind of environment. Increasingly, however, more of us are having to. Events and evolution have seen to that; jobs for life, pensionable age, borrowing, state support, personal safety and health, to name just a few, have all been deeply affected over the last few decades and exaggerated since 2007.

When we feel stress or threat, a simple human reflex is often to attack. We look to channel blame and seek a focus for our discomfort. We were, after all, promised security and certainty if we did as we were told and followed the paths mapped for us. So we did as we were guided and for huge numbers it didn't work out as planned: no job for life, no security, economic or otherwise, and as a result, our certainty has been undermined. A vast swathe of the global population is under stress and I believe that this has led to intense anger and hatred – a revolution against those who 'lied to us'.

This has inevitably bled into the education space and has led to a bit of a perfect storm. Teachers have for decades railed against constant interference, micromanagement, change and erosion of control. You just have to look at the numbers of educators who have suffered some form of stress-related illness or who have chosen, for the good of their sanity, to walk away from a career they loved. As with the hyper-divisive events around Trump and Brexit, powerful voices feed the stress and anger and help to channel blame by demonising certain figures, movements and beliefs. Hatred becomes the energy of reaction and the vehicle to attempt to regain control. Polarisation follows. The accelerant that is social media feeds the flames and here we are.

I urge us all, as educators, to come together and to spend a little more time exploring that which we have in common rather than that which divides us. I want us all to take inspiration from each other's energy and passion for education and for the future generations we have the privilege of working with. I do not want to bombard you with evidence and research or to manipulate either to find 'the truth', mainly because I don't believe there is one. Humankind is gloriously complex, organic, unpredictable and evolutionary, and that is why education is so frustratingly complex. There is no elegant solution, no neat and tidy answer, but there are pathways we can explore, given the right stimulus, the right questions, the right attitudes, and that is what I want us to do here. We have to draw a line under the anger and hatred, the debates sometimes fuelled by ego or control, and reboot our way forward.

Looking back on the last few years, has any of the name-calling, politicking or polarisation really made a difference in education? Has it helped us to move on and progress? Has it modelled the kind of behaviour we want and expect from our children? I don't think so. We may have seen movement in some data and in certain league tables, which is good, but is that really the main indicator of educational success a sophisticated society should focus on? Not everything of value can be measured or quantified through testing. As we come together as educators, I want us to look beyond the pressures and judgements of quantifiable data, to look deeper and with open-minded enquiry into what matters, why and what we can do about it collaboratively.

'Education is the most powerful weapon which you can use to change the world.'
Nelson Mandela (2003)

If this is the case, and I absolutely believe it is, then we need to start with an understanding of how we need the world to change.

It seems to me that we need, more than anything, to engender a sense of hope and possibility again. How many of our children dare to dream and how many of us are helping them to transform those dreams into aspirations? One thing is for sure: our children have been watching and processing the events of the last few years – the increasing anger, frustration and division. It worries them. There is a growing anxiety amongst young people. There is a lack of clarity around their own futures and too few role models exuding confidence or optimism on their behalf; to many, there appears to be no one fighting for them.

Now is our time. Educators have always been the bridges to tomorrow and now, more than ever, children need us to listen to them, to teach them, to raise their heads above the parapet and to develop in them the skills and belief they need to feel that they can control their own future. To do that, though, we need to regain that sense of collegiate purpose that some have been working hard to fragment.

One of the recurring phrases I have used over the last few years has been:

'Systems and structures change nothing; people do.'

This phrase is largely based on my time spent working in and observing complex organisations as they desperately try to transform and develop their capacity to function in such an exponentially changing environment. I have seen so many organisations across many fields – education, technology, finance, sports and entertainment – focus almost all of their time and resources on structures and shiny policies that, at best, have nothing more than a short-term impact. To change anything in a sustainable and truly effective way, you have to focus on the people and their context and understanding of why change is important. In education, we are often so busy delivering learning, or adopting a policy or some new thinking, gleaned from an expert or a training day, that to an extent we feel like part of the machine, not engineers of it. As a result, our students too feel like passive recipients of learning, rather than active participants.

A few years ago, Google started to explore the characteristics, skills and behaviours that worked best within the organisation. They wanted to use their vast ability to track and analyse performance to explore what levers had really made a difference. Initially, the results came as a bit of a surprise to the company's founders, Sergey Brin and Larry Page. Both men, being self-confessed tech geeks, believed that it was all about the STEM (science, technology, engineering and mathematics) geniuses they had been able to recruit, but the findings showed them something else, something just a little more human. The technical skills, which are so obviously important in an organisation like Google, came eighth in order of importance for the effectiveness of managers. The seven traits placed higher than technical skills in what they called the 'Project Oxygen' report (Morrison, 2012) were, in order:

- Be a good coach.
- Empower your team **(students)** and don't micromanage.
- Express interest in team members' **(students')** success and personal wellbeing.
- Don't be a coward: be productive and results-oriented.
- Be a good communicator and listen to your team **(students)**.
- Help your employees **(students)** with career development.
- Have a clear vision and strategy for the team **(class)**.

As you read through these, you will recognise that they are all the behaviours not just of good school leaders but of great teachers too and I don't believe that there is a single teacher, anywhere, who, whatever their philosophical view, would disagree that these are the key characteristics in a successful classroom or a thriving school. In brackets I have suggested some relevant changes for our context. As teachers and as leaders in our classrooms, we need to think about how we can apply these behaviours to create a sense of interaction and active participation amongst our students. I will return to these characteristics in Chapter 5.

Google followed this research up with 'Project Aristotle' (BlueEQ™, 2017), an exploration of what made the perfect team; the project was so called as a tribute to Aristotle's quote:

'The whole is greater than the sum of its parts.'

The researchers discovered that the outcomes were less dependent on who was in the team than on how the team worked together. The five key findings, in order, were:

- **Psychological safety:** Psychological safety refers to an individual's perception of the consequences of taking an interpersonal risk or a belief that a team, or in our context, a classroom, is safe for risk-taking in the face of being seen as ignorant, incompetent, negative or disruptive. In a team with high psychological safety, teammates feel safe to take risks around their team members. They feel confident that no one on the team will embarrass or punish anyone else for admitting a mistake, asking a question or offering a new idea.
- **Dependability:** On dependable teams, members reliably complete quality work on time (versus the opposite – shirking responsibilities).
- **Structure and clarity:** An individual's understanding of job expectations, the process for fulfilling these expectations and the consequences of one's performance are important for team effectiveness. Goals can be set at the

individual or group level, and must be specific, challenging and attainable. Google often uses objectives and key results (OKRs) to help set and communicate short- and long-term goals.

- **Meaning:** Finding a sense of purpose in either the work itself or the output is important for team effectiveness. The meaning of work is personal and can vary: financial security, supporting family, helping the team succeed or self-expression for each individual, for example.
- **Impact:** The results of one's work and the subjective judgement that your work is making a difference is important for teams. Seeing that one's work is contributing to the organisation's goals can help reveal impact.

For me, the findings of Project Aristotle can be profoundly important to us all, especially as teachers and school leaders. Let's take the first and most important quality of successful teams: **psychological safety**. This will not be the only time I talk about risk in this book but the vital importance highlighted here, of developing a culture of safety, where people feel confident enough to express themselves, to take risks, to innovate, to question, is clearly of primary importance to us all, yet I fear that it is the reverse of this that is the cultural norm for so many of us, both in reality and in virtual reality through social media. If you use social media for professional purposes, I ask you, urge you, to audit who you follow and ask yourself whether they are helping or hindering the development of a culture of psychological safety. It isn't, after all, just something for our classrooms – the behaviours and cultures have to flow through us first. In our schools and classrooms, we need to work hard to reframe the idea of mistake-making, error and failure, to ensure that neither educators nor students feel too intimidated by the need to succeed and therefore limit their ability to develop. We need to work hard at creating contexts where honesty is promoted and where the courage to admit a lack of knowledge or understanding is encouraged and supported.

In terms of **dependability**, we need to behave the same way we expect our students to behave; we must not hide from our responsibilities to others and allow ourselves to become siloed individually or in sub groups, either curricular or departmental. We must be supportive and always be aware of our roles and responsibilities in wider contexts. We must acknowledge that, as educators, we have a duty to consider every learner, everywhere, and we need to be as selfless as we can in that.

Ensuring **structure and clarity** around the setting of goals has always been a crucial part of a teacher's role, and how clear those goals and targets are has a real impact on the performance of our students. The same is true for us as teachers and as members of a staff and professional team. We must be prepared to accept and embrace challenge and to take on goals that are for the common good. As leaders, it is vital that goals and targets are contextualised so that all staff can see the value of the goal and their value to the process and in the outcome. To embrace a goal or a target, we all have to see and feel the relevance.

One of the great challenges for a teacher is to help our students find real **meaning** in what we teach and one of the greatest rewards is when they do. Contextualising learning is a holy grail and something that teachers should strive for in every element of their planning. It is also, of course, vital that we as teachers have clarity and context as to why we are working the way we are. It appears that so much of the frustration felt by so many teachers is that they have no clarity as to why they are being asked to spend so much of their time delivering what they are told to deliver. Having a sense of meaning about what you do and why you do it is central to believing that you have a purpose, and having a purpose means that you are far better equipped to drive on with a resilience and focus that can often define success.

The fifth and final key finding of Project Aristotle was around **impact**; I wonder whether we dwell too long in our jobs on what we've not done or achieved for fear of complacency. Do we give ourselves enough time or even simply permission to celebrate the good things that we do, not just in terms of figurative and data impact but also in terms of the human things that drew most of us to the profession in the first place: the child, whom you have made feel better about themselves after a lunchtime chat about a friendship group, a problem at home or a nasty social media exchange?

We live in a world where achievements must be externally validated to be of significance and that is more than just a shame. A few years ago, when I was writing my second book, *Change: Learn to Love It, Learn to Lead It,* I did some research on the traits of great people: people who have left an indelible mark on humanity. They all had a number of characteristics in common and, whether it was Maya Angelou, Ada Lovelace or Nelson Mandela, they all possessed a profound sense of higher purpose, something that drove them on and helped them to change the world.

Education needs us all, no matter what our philosophical position, to come together under our shared sense of higher purpose. We all have the right to and can make the world better for our kids. Whether you believe in the work of E. D. Hirsh or Maria Montessori, both wanted to use their expertise to improve the life chances of young people and so do I. Maybe, just maybe, we should spend our time more productively than trying to undermine their thinking and spend a little more time on asking how, despite our reflex, their thinking can be of use.

I have had the good fortune to spend a little time with Google and with organisations like them. When I mention that to some educators they castigate me, telling me that I shouldn't be associating with the immorality of tax-avoiding companies. I have real sympathy for that view, but I also believe that they have much to teach us, particularly around how to come together for a higher purpose. After all, Google wasn't founded to make billions; it was founded to 'Organize the world's information, make it accessible to all and by so doing, diminish evil.'

One of the many things I like about the culture in organisations like Google is what I call the culture of assumed excellence. It is a culture that feeds the characteristics highlighted in Project Oxygen and Project Aristotle. They assume that their people are committed, passionate and skilled in their work, and this leads to shared purpose and a commitment to succeed. There are disagreements and often heated debates about direction, research and development, and process, but energy is never wasted on trying to undermine colleagues. Instead, it is spent trying to understand them and to find a common ground on which to move forward.

This isn't a culture I have only seen in new tech businesses; I have seen it in really successful schools too and it is, I believe, the foundational challenge of great leadership. I worry, however, that there are some who assume incompetence in education and educators, and therefore spend their time proving that and also over-managing, in the belief that teachers and schools will only achieve if made to do so. Sometimes, I think that this attitude also bleeds down into our classrooms and our children. What we know about kids is that they are born as incredible learners, all of them; they have a natural curiosity and desire to know more. Yet so much time and energy is taken by some of our policy makers and those around them to construct systems to control kids first, in the belief that they are lazy or lack a desire to learn.

If we assume the worst, if we look for it and if we seek to undermine others in order to justify our own positions, are we not using really powerful skills in completely unproductive ways? Are we not, by dissipating the power and passion that drive us, only undermining the potential good we could do as a united body, with a common cause?

Start by finding common ground, trust in that and build from there!

Over the last ten years, I have visited and written about some stunning examples of where finding a common purpose has made a profound difference to the life chances of children. Medellin, for example, in Colombia, was a place torn apart during the reign of terror and corruption perpetuated by Pablo Escobar. As a city, it realised that if it was to build a future for itself, it needed to unify a people fragmented by Escobar and by massive inequality. It decided to work towards becoming a technological hub in Latin America. To do that, it worked hard to bring together the education, cultural and business sectors and to invest heavily in the poorest hillside communities on the outskirts of the city. It provided infrastructure that meant that travel to and from the centre of Medellin was easier and affordable. It built cultural facilities and high-quality learning environments in the heart of the most deprived areas and it invested heavily in those areas' schools. The philosophy was simple: if we can bring the city to the people and make the hope and vision tangible, we trust in their natural desire to succeed. Today Medellin is a rapidly transforming place, one of the most dynamic and inspirational places I have ever had the privilege of visiting. It is by no means a fairy tale and it still has its disputes and a myriad of issues, but there is a growing trust and belief – a commonality of cause that is overcoming those challenges. It is a community, working together for the betterment of all, especially its children.

When you look at the world's most dynamic education systems, they all have something in common: their hunger to learn. In my time, I have worked in most of them, South Korea, China, Singapore, Finland and New Zealand included. The first thing you notice, as a presenter and trainer, is their lack of cynicism. They are open to learning, to being challenged to think and explore new ideas and approaches. Their first reflex is not to undermine or disprove but to engage. The default setting is not 'I don't agree so I will undermine you', but 'That's interesting. What can I learn from that?'

Common ground does not mean universal agreement, blind acceptance or complete, unconditional support but it does mean starting from a position of shared goals and vision and it means building a position of trust from there – an environment governed by respect and a belief that everyone's views and experiences are of value.

If we want to help our children build and populate a better world then, surely, peace has to be at its heart; good things come from peace. Co-operation must surely be our default and I ask you all to read the remainder of this book in that spirit. In the words of the great Martin Luther King Jr (1963):

> 'Peace cannot be kept by force; it can only be achieved by understanding. Darkness cannot drive out darkness; only light can do that. Hate cannot drive out hate; only love can do that.'

2
It takes a village

'No one can whistle a symphony. It takes a whole orchestra to play it.'
H. E. Luccock

In 1986, shortly after being fired by Apple, Steve Jobs bought a small computer company called Pixar. He wanted to use the entity to create a new type of film-making organisation that brought together previously separate skills, disciplines and expertise. He wanted to create a unique collaboration that would convey a fresh energy and creativity to the process of storytelling and making movies. At the turn of the millennium the company was relocated to purpose-built premises on the site of a former Del Monte canning factory in Emeryville, California. The campus was originally planned to have three distinct buildings, which would house the computer scientists, animators and executives independently. Jobs, however, vetoed that plan and instead created one extraordinary space connected by a vast atrium. When asked about the decision, Ed Catmull, the then president of Pixar, explained:

'The philosophy behind this design is that it's good to put the most important function at the heart of the building. Well, what's our most important function? It's the interaction of our employees. That's why Steve put a big empty space there. He wanted to create an open area for people to always be talking to each other.'

Jobs then ensured that everyone spent time in the atrium by putting all the communal services there, from the post box to the café and the gifts shops, meaning that people had to gravitate to that collaborative meeting point. He knew that creativity could only happen through collaboration, and collaboration needed people to come together, people who would otherwise exist in their unique silos. He knew that innovation starts with human interaction.

Brad Bird, the director of the films *The Incredibles* and *Ratatouille* said, 'The atrium initially might seem like a waste of space. But Steve realised that when people run into each other, when they make eye contact, things happen.'

The Latin phrase that hangs over the entrance at Pixar reads:

'Alienus Non-Diutius'

Translated this means 'alone no longer'. (Lehrer, 2011)

When I left my headship in 2007, schools in the UK were encouraged to share, to collaborate and to learn from each other's great practice. The process wasn't perfect and had taken many years to evolve. I have to confess that the chance to work with other schools and to learn from other professionals was one of the greatest privileges of the job. I was inspired so many times by seeing incredible work in other schools. Over the last ten years that privilege has expanded further afield, allowing me the extraordinary opportunity to see the work of educators from around the world. Many of those experiences I explored in the second edition of my first book, *Creating Tomorrow's Schools Today*. The thing that has always struck me has been the generosity and humility of the passionate professionals I have spent time with, from the courage shown in Pakistan by educators prepared to risk everything in order to provide an open and equitable education, to the vision of the entire community in Medellin, Colombia, which I mentioned in Chapter 1 (page 15), who have together worked tirelessly to bring a fragmented and socially damaged city together in order to give all of their young people a future in a globally successful environment.

The last few years, however, have seen a shift, not just in education but across many sectors, as they return to a belief in the traditional view of competition to drive success. To understand it and how it has resurfaced in education policy is, I believe, important in order to understand the challenges we have to work with, to ensure that collaboration is preserved at the heart of our system.

The simple philosophy behind competition is that rivalry amongst sellers increases resources, efficiency and choice for the consumer. As education has become increasingly conflated with the 'war on talent', or the global competition for hiring and retaining the most educated and skilled employees, governments have focused on the academic performance data provided by organisations such as the OECD. Many governments, especially in the UK and the US, have seen the costs of public education rise, with what they see as no real progress in student performance and a perception that other jurisdictions such as Shanghai, Singapore and South Korea are besting us. Market theory or competition has been the key behind the evolution of free schools in the UK and charter schools in the US, both of which show very patchy evidence of large-scale success.

What I believe is that education has to be about more than one model and one offer; it must embrace diversity and create expansive opportunities. It must work harder to develop brilliant vocational opportunities as well as academic ones and, above all, it must remain relevant to the world around us and, more importantly, to the one evolving for our children. To do that successfully will require a commitment to the nurturing and development of inter and intra relationships.

In my opinion, competition in the sector promotes not just inequality but, worse, a disconnect. It can not only set professionals against each other, as we saw in the previous chapter, but it can also narrow the vision and strategic development of the offer. You just have to see the struggles that traditionally run businesses have had in the fast-moving and developing economies of the 21st century, fuelled by the exponentially influential technological revolution. So much of the work I have been involved in outside of education has been in helping competition-focused businesses recalibrate and develop collaborative cultures both internally and externally, in order to stimulate the innovative outlooks required in such a fast-moving environment.

Maybe we all need to be a little bit more Pixar in our lives, and in this chapter, I want to explore both the barriers to and the steps towards a better collaborative culture.

Trust

Collaboration will always suffer if there is an underlining lack of respect and trust. Many teachers feel vulnerable and actually quite insecure about their own practice, even the greatest ones, and this means that as a profession, we are sometimes nervous of sharing. I remember my own feeling of fear if I was having a lesson observed by a senior colleague, often completely unwarranted but there none the less. We are a profession that feels under scrutiny all of the time; there is definitely an overriding perception of assumed incompetence – that place where we feel that our performance is heavily managed in order to evidence performance.

It is really important to underline at this point that according to the Ipsos MORI (2017a) Veracity Index, teachers are the most trusted of all professions after doctors and nurses, with an 87 per cent rating. To give some context, journalists have a 27 per cent trust rating and politicians a 17 per cent score.

As teachers, many feel under a constant level of scrutiny that almost requires them to evidence their ability to do the job on a daily basis. This is not new and not unique to education. Many organisations run on the competitive model are done so using a philosophy of assumed incompetence, so as well as being based on the premise that staff will only do their best if they are managed to do so, it is also the model that believes in competition between colleagues in order to drive up performance. It doesn't take a lot to realise that this philosophy does not easily foster collaboration; people are protective of their own ideas and practice and some will even try to undermine their colleagues to 'shine'. There is an argument that in some environments this may work – high-performance sales for example. However, as a profession, we are in the middle of a perfect storm. There is a lack of trust at policy level, which bleeds into our classrooms and, as we know, leads to the fight or flight reflex that humans feel when under threat and also in a system that is increasingly designed to be hyper-competitive.

The policy of divide and rule (or divide and conquer) is an ancient political strategy used through history and has been used at many phases of modern management and often in the public sector. Some politicians have been very skilled at sowing discord to gain a power base. I feel we are in such a phase in many of the education jurisdictions I visit currently, and it is one of the main reasons for my opening plea that we find a way to work together, with shared goals and in peace.

For what it's worth, when I became a teacher, I felt it was a little like committing to the Hippocratic Oath that the medical profession stands by. As qualified and committed educators, I believe that it is our responsibility to directly and indirectly support the learning of all children, everywhere. Our job is of course to do the very best for the students in our care, but it is also to recognise our moral responsibility to all young people. As with medics, it is vital that we share our knowledge and expertise, our experiences and our processes for the benefit of society. For those in the profession who feel frustrated and even angry at the way we are managed from above, the best way to fight back is through collaboration – to refuse to be divided and to hold on to our mutuality through respect and shared trust.

In any profession there will always be heightened debate, disagreement and the clash of mindsets and so there should be; as we know better than perhaps anyone, learning and human development only happen through challenge: the ability to question and to be questioned, to be curious and to be hungry to keep developing. That of course cannot happen within set comfort zones or protected practice. Great teachers are always challenging their own thinking and reflecting on their methodology. Simply surrounding yourself with likeminded people who reinforce your views cannot be healthy, although it is totally understandable in a low-trust environment. Whilst I love the opportunities that social media has given us, one of the concerns I have with it, as I suggested in Chapter 1, is that some users tend to exist inside echo chambers and those who don't tend to 'go to war' with people who provoke or challenge their viewpoint.

We all need to develop the maturity and self-confidence to accept that by its nature, education is challenging, that because we are dealing in the gloriously organic and unpredictable world of human beings, there is no one solution, methodology or process that will work for all. As with everything in life, our viewpoints are moulded by our own experiences and they then influence our mindset. I think that what I have enjoyed most about the last few years of my professional life has been to have the opportunity to experience other contexts, other people's contexts and other environments that provide endless provocation to my own thinking and ultimately to my mindset. I used to reflexively try to find flaws in people and their positions if they were different from mine, but now I have learnt to embrace that difference and use it to challenge my own views of the world. That doesn't mean I will always fall in and agree but it does mean that I spend less time and energy protecting my stance and more time and energy trying to evolve it. I used to tell my students that, in order to grow, you have to be the first to challenge your own thinking.

As you will have already seen, I do worry that in some quarters social media has only helped to drive division in education, a little like ice expanding in a crack in the road. It concerns me that there is an amplification of 'confirmation bias' or, as Professor David Perkins of Harvard University calls it, 'mysid', short for 'myside bias', referring to a preference for 'my' side of an issue. It relates to the almost human reflex that allows us to hear only what we want to or to interpret and manipulate information, evidence and data so that it supports our own hypotheses. It is apparently particularly prevalent in emotionally charged issues; I can think of few more charged than education for those in and around it, and as a result it leads to frequent polarisation. The selective processing at the heart of confirmation bias and the echo chamber it can create serve to reinforce beliefs and therefore lead to overconfidence. In the age of social media, this is further amplified by the people you follow and who follow you, most of whom support and reinforce your views. Confirmation bias is often most commonly seen in politics and traditionally hierarchical organisations. As I've said, one of the reasons I have largely retreated from the debate online is because of the increased polarisation and confirmation bias that surround the education debate. It saddens me how deeply personal and territorial it can be. We need to be conscious of and sensitive to the problem and work harder to rebalance the debates so that they are more constructive. Imagine what we could only accomplish if we pooled our wisdom, experience and passion? Ultimately, we must be prepared to be challenged, to frequently interrogate our own beliefs and to have the confidence to admit when we see a better way than our own.

Knowledge deficit

I first heard the term knowledge deficit in a medical context, when talking with a friend who works in the field of research science. It is a major issue in health care and relates to the challenge of educating the mass populous in medical science, so that they can better understand the management of their own health and the research behind the recommendations. There is a reticence on the side of some in the scientific community to engage with the public beyond their own research and there is even a tension between scientific researchers and practitioners. This is largely because scientists often feel threatened and vulnerable to the perceived ignorance of people operating outside of their field, who try to hold them to account. For some scientists they regard the idea of knowledge deficit as convenient, almost comfortable, believing that citizens, including decision makers, political representatives and journalists, simply need to be informed. There is arrogance in some who work within scientific research that leads to a belief that any further discourse or collaboration would be arduous and beneath them. There is a friction though, because many people outside of the bubble feel that they can and should contribute to scientific development and that actually the outside perspective is vital for genuine evolution and progress. Many people feel that for the scientific community to believe that all lay people are the same, with the same level of knowledge or understanding, is more than just patronising; it actually prevents real opportunity and the stimulus of fresh perspectives. Those same people argue that if scientists were more interactive and inclusive, their standing would not only improve but engagement in proactive health care would also rise. We have seen some small evidence of this in the last few years when some medical professionals have tried, at times clumsily, to impact on childhood obesity through schools.

Taking a step back though, listening to my friend made me think about education and schooling directly. We must do more to break down the 'walls' around our schools and find ways to actively promote the direct involvement of parents and the wider community in education development, not just in the cosy and controlled delivery of reading schemes or parent–teacher associations. As educators we must realise and respect the value that the wider community can bring to the evolution of education. Some in our profession, who, if we are honest, behave a little like the scientists I have described, have a tendency to hold people, citizens, who are outside the profession, at arm's length with a mixture of vulnerability and arrogance. I am not undermining the required skill, training and professionalism of teachers, as critics within medical science aren't, but we need to be more open to the relevance of the experiences and expertise our communities can bring to education and its evolution. Many of our parents, for example, are in the modern workforce at varying levels and those who aren't will have interesting and challenging perspectives on why not. Companies and organisations in our communities have fantastic insight into the kinds of skills, knowledge, attributes and attitudes our students need to develop. Third-sector agencies involved in the environment, poverty and health care could have highly relevant input into how we educate our future adult citizens. These are issues that I explore further in Chapter 3.

In 2014, the European Molecular Biology Organization published a paper exploring 'Thinking outside the "knowledge deficit" box' (Pouliot and Godbout, 2014). The paper looked to find a progression for the scientific community to move towards a more inclusive collaborative approach and it cited a three-stage process that I believe could be relevant to us:

1. **The deficit model:** This is the current position where the science community produces a uni-directional discourse based on the belief that the public are an undifferentiated mass. This leads to information that is produced by the scientists only and is justified because of the perceived inability for 'citizens' to understand: the knowledge deficit.

2. **The public debate model:** This is the first stage in progress, where the science community acknowledges that the public have a differentiated ability and desire to participate and that their views and ideas can add value, creating a bi-directional discourse. As a result, knowledge is produced by scientists but enriched through the viewpoints of citizens and there is a forum for the public to express their views.

3. **The co-production model:** This is the final and most exciting stage, with a fully matured, bi-directional discourse allowing the production and development of knowledge to be genuine collaboration between scientific and lay groups, promoting equity of involvement, respect and participation.

Within the context of education, there are perhaps three perceived groups that need to find a direction of travel towards co-production. There are many who perceive that government decides policy and controls the message for parents, educators and students. Whilst we know that this is only partly true, we do need to work towards a more inclusive and interactive process of education development, one that encourages input from the wider community through organised public debate and discourse, so that finally, we can arrive at a system of genuine co-production. I was recently invited to participate in an event convened by HRH Prince of Wales, to explore how we can ensure that the arts remain a core element of education and of all children's experience. The meeting was inspirational because it brought together educators, policy makers and arts professionals: three central stakeholders who spent time together, exploring three simple yet crucial questions. What can schools do to improve the provision of the arts, what can policy makers do and what can the industry do? The result has led not just to a pledge and commitment but also to new connections and collaborations that will make a real difference over the coming months and years.

For me, this idea of moving towards a greater sense of shared responsibility must be desirable and can only be of benefit to us all and, most importantly, to our children. There will never be a whole village involved in education until there is a greater focus on democracy and partnership – partnership that shares not only the process but the responsibility for it and, perhaps most significantly, for its outcomes.

Aligning common goals

One of the most common inhibitors to genuine collaboration is a lack of alignment around the goals and this, above all things, is the most significant barrier for greater progress towards a collaborative approach. Increasingly over the last few years, I think that education has been so confused by endless top-down interventions, restructuring and financial constraints that we have become largely reactive in our development. As a result, whilst our sense of purpose burns bright and is the driving force of most of us in education, it has been diluted, and with it, I sense that the goals that should define our process are disparate and even conflicting across the many stakeholders involved. This is by no means an exhaustive list but the current drivers include: social mobility and equity of opportunity; economics; childcare; reduction of state control; increased accountability; ideologies that include education as a social right and as a means to reduce state dependency; public–private partnerships; knowledge acquisition; preparation for active citizenship and to compete with the Asian market... I could go on. I would hope, though, that, as I have mentioned before, we can all agree that at the heart of an education system is the welfare and development of our young people so that they can live productive and fulfilling lives for the betterment of themselves and of society.

On a micro level, though, the pressures that many teachers find themselves with can see personal perspectives cloud a corporate sense of mission. Some of our colleagues just want to survive the day; some want promotion; some just want to revel in the joy of teaching. I guess the challenge is that there are so many stakeholders and voices pulling us in so many directions: colleagues, parents, unions, school leaders, governing boards, inspectorates, students... and again the list can go on. All of these forces can and have inhibited genuine opportunities for collaboration and particularly for proactive collaboration.

At this point I must celebrate the rise of the 'unconference' or TeachMeets as they have become known in the UK – EdCamps in the US. These are events organised for teachers by teachers. They are an incredible source of inspiration and collaboration for many. They illustrate a clear desire from teachers to want to rid themselves of the noise, to focus on teaching and learning, to share their experiences and to be better for their students. Sadly, as resources and budgets have become increasingly stretched, real opportunities for high-quality professional development have diminished and, more damagingly, they are still pulled in the endless directions of travel highlighted above.

We desperately need to agree common goals and values before we can possibly hope to draw society together and work towards full collaboration, and whilst there is a huge responsibility of leadership here, which I will address in Chapter 9, we must recognise that we all need to work harder on finding common ground.

One thing we can all activate quickly is a commitment to each other, internally, to spend more time talking and sharing. Schools are such complex places, often filled with so many silos, splintered by year group and subject. The Jobs-driven Pixar philosophy of bringing people together informally, in a shared space, often without agenda and just to see what happens, is such a powerful one and is something I am seeing increasingly across a number of sectors and organisations. There is a growing realisation in major companies that by functioning entirely in their own silos, departments can actually work against each other as they try to move the business forward. I have seen it for myself: situations where simple communication and a desire to find common purpose could solve major issues. In schools, for example, it must be all teachers, across all subjects and all year groups, who must explicitly share responsibility for the development of literacy and numeracy as well as, for example, teamwork, creativity and problem-solving. Surely, if we want to embed a modern foreign language, we should endeavour to use that language occasionally in all classes. If we want to develop research skills, we should ensure subjects are coordinated to support and reinforce each other.

We must all be prepared to leave our comfort zones, our silos and our egos behind if we are to further evolve the cultures of generosity, reflection, sharing and trust that open the pathway to better collaboration. I know that it is almost a cliché, but it really does take a village to raise a child. Collaboration isn't easy, but it has to be worth fighting for. There are those who are glad of fragmentation, of a blurring of purpose and of polarisation. At the start of this book, I promised not to be too political or adversarial but if we are to reclaim education from the policy makers and ideologues who have worked so hard to create discord in a profession where so many feel isolated and impotent, we must use the one lever we have to create strength, unity and courage, and that is collaboration; we must bring people, communities and organisations together. It is not about us finding complete consensus of opinion or even process, but it is about us finding a consensus of purpose, one that excludes no one, even said policy makers. What we have to all seek to achieve is equity of voice, respect and a commitment to develop.

People trust us and that places us in a strong position to lead powerful collaboration with everyone who has an interest in the future of education, with a community that together, with our shared knowledge, experience and expertise, can ensure our children have the best possible start to their future. So, let's exploit it for good.

3
Beyond the walls

'Alone we can do so little. Together we can do so much.'
Helen Keller *(as quoted in Lash, 1997)*

As I mentioned in the introduction, I have to confess that one of the reasons for me writing this book came from the motivation I gained following that perfectly innocent remark from the young teacher I met in Edinburgh, who observed that many people thought that I had left education behind, having 'crossed over' into the corporate and business world. I can understand why that could be the perception but it is simply not the case for two reasons.

Firstly, at least 50 per cent of my work is still in and around education, admittedly not at a curricular level but around human development, leadership and change. Secondly, and more importantly, I don't see that there is a 'crossing over', some dramatic dividing line or Trump-like wall that separates education from anything else. I am well aware that there is a perception amongst some that there is and indeed there are a few who believe that there should be.

Over the last ten years, I have observed at first hand the impact of an increasingly changing and uncertain world on people both in education and far beyond it. I left headship at the start of the maelstrom that was the financial crisis when the impact of the shifts in the modern world caused by changes through globalisation, economic shifts and working patterns accelerated beyond our control, leaving us all in a state of shock. People, good people, were left without jobs, homes and, in some cases, basic human decency. Services, organisations and companies that had spent a great deal of time and money developing change programmes found themselves unable to cope with what was blowing up around them and many started to explore why.

I have often asked myself how and why I was able to transition from primary school teacher to 'leadership expert' across a number of fields and disciplines. I look for complex factors but in truth I keep coming back to the same thing: I was a teacher.

One of the most important things I have learnt over the last decade is that the best teachers are, without a doubt, the world's foremost experts in human leadership. Don't take my word for it. Both the second and 36th presidents of the United

States of America, John Adams and Lyndon Johnson, started out as teachers. US Senator Elizabeth Warren started her career as a special needs teacher. Canadian Prime Minister Justin Trudeau taught primary school maths. Legendary Dutch soccer managers Rinus Michels and Guus Hiddink were both teachers, as was World Cup-winning rugby union coach Sir Clive Woodward. History was literally changed by teachers, by author and civil rights campaigner Harriet Beecher Stowe and by Annie Sullivan, who not only taught Helen Keller but inspired both Andrew Carnegie and Alexander Graham Bell.

Sometimes I wonder if teachers are so busy doing, and in particular giving to their students and communities, and are so often under assault from various elements of the media and certain politicians that they have lost sight of the incredible talents, knowledge and skill sets they possess. I want to remind you of some of the most important.

1. Great teachers know how to create a strong culture.

They have the ability to create dynamic and vibrant environments where students feel safe, respected and stimulated. They know how to inspire even the most hardened student on a wet Wednesday afternoon and they can transform the attitudes of students who lead complex and challenging home lives – lives that most of us can barely imagine. Through their authenticity and skill, they make every life they touch matter.

2. Great teachers know how to set high expectations.

They encourage students to believe in more and aim higher; they raise their students' sense of aspiration and value, and drive them to achieve way beyond their own expectations. The safe and respectful climate they produce is crucial to accomplishing that.

3. Great teachers prioritise what really matters.

Teachers know how to personalise and prioritise the needs of each and every child. They possess levels of emotional intelligence, and through deep knowledge and understanding of their students and of their job, they are able to sift through the thousands of variables in order to respond to need in highly targeted ways.

4. Great teachers plan.

They know how to deliver complex programmes and processes in logical and coherent ways, flexible enough to adapt yet clear enough to succeed.

5. Great teachers execute.

Every day, teachers execute their plans irrespective of the variables thrown in their direction and they do so with an undying loyalty to their students and their purpose. Their focus is laser-like and unshakeable.

6. Great teachers learn constantly.

The very best teachers follow a never-ending pursuit to be better. They analyse their own performance and critically assess how to improve. The truly great ones are confident enough to collaborate and share strengths and weaknesses and they are as committed to learning as they are to teaching. The fact that they themselves are passionate about learning and development inspires those around them to be the same.

7. Great teachers persevere.

Under often intense pressure and scrutiny, teachers always bounce back; whether it was a difficult lesson, a tough meeting with a parent or trouble with a colleague, they always shine with their students. Regardless of what may be going on at home, they will always be professional, put their students first and put on a show; great teachers exhibit levels of focus and courage that exude energy, belief and trust.

8. Great teachers are resourceful.

They may not know it but teachers are incredibly entrepreneurial; often starved of resources, funds and equipment, they always find a way. They solve problems and meet challenges in highly creative and innovative ways. When a great teacher has an idea, they will find a way to see it through. Obstacles are there to be overcome; that belief is then seen, often profoundly, in their students.

9. Great teachers empathise.

Most importantly of all, teachers know and understand their students on a deeply human level. They have levels of emotional intelligence that are awe-inspiring. Every nuance of a child's behaviour is processed and understood. Great teachers know that their success and ultimately that of their students comes from their ability to work out the blockers, drivers and motivations of every one of their students, no matter what their background or behaviour. The split-second shifts in mood, tone and action required to inspire over 30 complex individuals in every hour of every day is extraordinary and teachers do it naturally.

Now, if you compare that list to the findings of Project Aristotle discussed in Chapter 1, you can see a striking similarity, and we teachers know that we have been doing these things for literally hundreds of years, long before Google even existed let alone researched them.

As a profession we need to be secure and self-confident enough to know that we are experts not only in our field but generically in the field of human leadership and development. However, we must also be secure and confident enough to understand that one of our own personal and professional traits needs to be utilised more: great teachers learn constantly.

We do and the very best of us have an insatiable appetite for learning, but we need to be prepared to learn from and with people and organisations beyond our normal experience, and this is where, I think, as a profession, we can improve. It is true of any organisation or industry that, when placed under pressure, usually to improve output and results, the people in that organisation focus on delivering what they are measured by, what they are rewarded for and what they get to keep their jobs because of. Our schools globally have come under increasing scrutiny and stress as the 'war for talent' grows – as markets become increasingly competitive and as countries fight for investment and edge. Our children are seen as the resource that attracts investment and that resource needs to be highly educated in order to demonstrate potential. I do not say this because I like it or because I endorse it but it is a fact of life and I have to confess that I want my children to grow up in a place where there is opportunity, optimism and hope and, to put it bluntly, that is far more likely in an environment where there is social and economic stability. We need to be aware of these drivers if we are to understand why policy makers are driving education the way they are. Again, I will talk about policy and practice in more detail as we progress but for now, if we take this as a reality then we can understand one of the key reasons why schools, teachers and school leaders are becoming increasingly insular. We are under threat and when we are under threat we retreat, hunker down and try to protect ourselves and those in our care. Most teachers are desperate to do a good job for their students and they want to be allowed the space, resource and freedom to do exactly that. However, the feeling that many have is that we are being attacked from all angles and so the classroom has become a refuge and our knowledge and expertise our comfort.

There is also, of course, the economic strain on schools as we experience the continuing fallout of the financial crisis of 2007/08 and also the financial impact of increasingly fragmented systems. This means that schools do not have the funds to spend on high levels of professional development for staff, relying on running it in-house or at low cost. The opportunities for teachers to step out of school are limited by the lack of money available to pay for cover. I am well aware that schools today are finding it hard to find the funds to cover staff who are ill, let alone for professional development.

So we have a perfect storm: a profession measured by fixed and very limited outcomes and a diminishing opportunity to fund professional development. There are also some, as I have said already, who regard education as a place where children should be insulated from the world beyond, and schools should be places that cele-brate learning for learning's sake.

What all of that means is that increasingly there is a divide between what is happening in our schools and what young people are faced with when they leave education. In January 2018, at the Davos World Economic Forum, the following concerns, from a number of globally renowned experts, were raised about the future of work and skills. These underline the challenge for education trends globally.

Firstly, the McKinsey Global Institute stated that their research suggested robots could replace 800 million jobs by 2030. Jack Ma, founder of the Chinese multi-national e-commerce giant Alibaba Group, said, 'If we do not change the way we teach, 30 years from now, we're going to be in trouble […] The knowledge-based approach of 200 years ago would fail our kids, who would never be able to compete with machines. Children should be taught soft skills like independent thinking, values and team-work.' The World Economic Forum agreed, suggesting that a 'skills revolution' could open up a multitude of new opportunities.

This was supported by Minouche Shafik, Director of the London School of Economics, in a session entitled 'Saving economic globalization from itself', in which she said, 'Anything that is routine or repetitive will be automated.' Shafik also spoke of the importance of 'the soft skills, creative skills. Research skills, the ability to find information, synthesise it, make something of it.' She went on to suggest that 'overhauling our education system will be essential to fixing the fractures in our societies and avoiding a tilt towards populism. It's no accident that the people who voted for populist parties around the world are people with by-and-large low levels of education. It's not because they're stupid, it's because they're smart. They've figured out this system will not be in their favour.'

Secondly, Fabiola Gianotti, a particle physicist, Director General of CERN and the woman in charge of the Large Hadron Collider as well as other Big Science projects, said: 'We need to break the cultural silos. Too often people put science and the humanities, or science and the arts, in different silos. They are the highest expression of the curiosity and creativity of humanity […] For me, I was a very curious child; I wanted to answer the big questions of how the universe works. My humanities and my music studies have contributed to what I am today as a scientist as much as my physics studies.'

What I find encouraging from this is the clear point of connection between educators and people working in the world beyond it. Firstly, we all want to prepare our children for the future; we all want that future to be a bright and optimistic place, maybe better than the world we find ourselves in today. I find Minouche Shafik's comment about populism particularly stimulating and pro-vocative and it is strongly reinforced by Barack Obama's views on education, which I discuss in Chapter 10. It highlights for me so much of what I have seen and heard as I've travelled around the world and through political and social systems: a growing view that we are educated to believe in and search out cer-tainties, certainties that for a growing number simply don't exist any longer and are leading to higher levels of disillusion and anger amongst perfectly rational and educated people.

Maybe, therefore, one of our challenges is this: to understand that as educators our job is not to teach children how to survive in the world but to help prepare them to thrive in it and, if we are to do that, then we need to be sure that we are aware of it, in order to help them to take ownership of it.

For many of us who work in education, however, the skills discussed in these quotes can seem quite abstract because some of us have never seen what they look like deployed in a dynamic, modern workplace. When I was a headteacher, in more economically secure times than these, I encouraged my staff to take professional development time in local businesses and services so that they could observe modern workplaces and environments, to help them crystallise what exactly 'soft skills' were and how we as expert educators could develop them in the context of the classroom. I wanted my teachers to feel informed about what the world was like and evolving into for our students.

The most important thing I've learnt over the last ten years about the context here is that we are not poles apart; the 'divide' between educators and employers is, for the most part, fabricated but because there is the perception of a divide, there is friction, suspicion and ignorance, which helps no one. Of course we could spend days, weeks, even years arguing as to why the two realms are incompatible, putting huge intellectual energy into constructing or reinforcing our positions, or we could spend a little longer finding that mutuality and working from it.

When I first stepped out into the world of business and industry and found myself in front of corporate audiences, I certainly faced a baptism of fire. One of my first non-education events was at the headquarters of RBS near Edinburgh. It was in the heart of the crisis and RBS was at the eye of the UK storm. I wasn't really sure what to expect – maybe a load of Italian-suited, 'coked-up' drunks, wheel spinning their way around a gold-plated courtyard in a throaty Ferrari.

Perception…

As I arrived, my initial thought was one of 'I knew it!' I drove up to the front gates to be met by high levels of security. I thought it was primarily there to keep the screaming hoards out and to protect the evil bankers from the reality of their ways. I was wrong. It turns out that the primary reason for the huge security presence was to prevent the workforce from marching out and throwing themselves off the nearby bridge, which apparently had been happening at an increasingly alarming rate. The vast majority of the workforce inside the campus weren't high-flying, vacuous types at all. They were a workforce on wages similar to those of teachers, who cared passionately about each other, their jobs and their clients; many were on the front line, having to help the distressed, who were losing their homes, their pensions, their security and many their livelihoods, whilst they themselves weren't sure whether they had a job to return to the following day. They too were victims, under huge duress based on their own powerlessness.

The following year, whilst working in Madrid, I remember being in a taxi, driving through the city centre and seeing hundreds of young people sat by the roadside, many with looks of despair and helplessness. It turns out that many were unemployed graduates and many, too, young men and women who had lost their jobs as a result of the collapse of the Spanish construction industry. Prior to the collapse, construction in Spain was booming, as we now know, built on very fragile economic foundations, but, as a result, many young people were encouraged to leave school in order to learn a craft and get into the building industry, which, it appeared, was a land of milk and honey. Thousands and thousands took up the advice in pursuit of certainty and when the crunch hit, the jobs crumbled away.

As educators, we cannot insulate ourselves from the world or pretend that we have no role to play in it. Similarly, we cannot endeavour to protect our students from it. We must do all that we can to prepare our children for it and to do that, we need to find ways to understand it and then to use our expertise to create learning opportunities for them.

In the previous chapter I talked at length about the invocation of the famous old African saying: 'It takes a village to raise a child.' I want to stress again the importance of regarding ourselves as the meeting house at the centre of that village and to embrace all members of the wider society to help us find a way forward.

We can start at a very local level of course. I have seen so many great examples of using local opportunities for mutual learning, shared experiences and genuine partnership. Take school governors and board members, for example – people with a wealth of experience beyond the school gates, many of whom work in interesting and diverse environments; opportunities to ask them about their challenges or to observe their workplace make for really stimulating experiences. Contacting local businesses or services too is so easy to do.

This is not a one-way street though. I have, over the years, met so many managers and leaders in business and industry who want to know how to get the best out of their new workforce – generations that think and behave very differently to previous ones, partly because of technology and partly because of the social environments they grow up in. Forward-thinking employers are not spending their time simply criticising or writing off young people as lazy, workshy, snowflakes or anything else. They can see the potential and want to know how to realise it. Working with a major news organisation some years ago, I was asked to participate in a think tank exploring how to make their news service more accessible and desirable to young people. We spent ages talking about interactivity and social activism. It was something I felt, as an educator and someone who had spent years crafting learning for kids with low-attention spans and an on-demand mentality, I could really contribute to. I am only one teacher; most would know exactly how to do the same.

As a profession we must work hard to regain our own confidence and sense of worth, of value. Others see it in us. It is why, despite the constant attacks, teachers are the second most trusted profession in the world after doctors. We are genuine experts – high-level professionals – and we must be more proactive in proving it. So maybe the challenge lies in responding to one of the key characteristics of successful teams, as identified in Project Aristotle (see Chapter 1, page 12): psychological safety. As mentioned previously, psychological safety refers to an individual's perception of the consequences of taking an interpersonal risk or a belief that a team, or in our context, a classroom, is safe for risk-taking in the face of being seen as ignorant, incompetent, negative or disruptive. In a team with high psychological safety, teammates feel safe to take risks around their team members. They feel confident that no one on the team will embarrass or punish anyone else for admitting a mistake, asking a question or offering a new idea. We need to see this finding as a challenge because we can only grasp the opportunities of wider collaboration if we can create, in ourselves, that feeling of psychological safety, so that we can use our voices, our experiences and our expertise in the wider community. As educators, we have so much to offer society and the more we demonstrate that, the more respect we can cultivate.

After the financial crisis of 2007/08, many organisations and leading economists warned of a reflex action that would lead to individual countries returning to an era of economic protectionism: the theory or practice of shielding a country's domestic industries from foreign competition by taxing imports. This certainly seems to be coming to pass, led by the US and also in a post-Brexit Europe. It stems from the lack of certainty, trust and stability we have all experienced over the last decade and is based on that simple human reflex linked to fight or flight. In economic terms the fear is this: that a resurgence of trade protectionism would not only significantly impair the global recovery process by further hampering trade flows and global demand but it would also reduce the global growth potential in the long run and, as a result, have long-term disruptive implications for the world economy.

As educators we must take the lead in ensuring that an educational protectionism doesn't take root and have a similar impact on our children and their futures. We must have the courage to lead beyond our classrooms and take the initiative in allowing and enabling partnership and collaboration instead. So for partnership and collaboration to flourish we need to create climates that take account of the following simple rules about collaboration:

- We must appreciate that people from other cultures and experiences will have different skills and methods of working. It will cause a situation of constant friction and tension if we don't accept that and compromise on it. We must all be open minded enough not to judge and reject but to find common ground.
- Utilise the skills and experiences that are specific to that person or organisation. Recognise each other's areas of expertise and be willing to sit back and let the other take the lead. Trust is the key.
- Do not be afraid to express your feelings, doubts or concerns, but do not become lost in them either. Keep the lines of communication open and equal between collaborators.
- If your collaborative relationship is built on friendship, mutual respect and trust then the work is enjoyable and productive.

When you think of life as a narrative and the various stages in it as chapters (school is one chapter, as is work), you need to connect both to help the creation of a story that makes sense. If we do not do more to connect the two, for too many of our children, education will appear abstract and, for many in their adult lives, irrelevant. If we are to create the culture of lifelong learning, which has never been more important, then we need to make sure that as adults, our students see the power and value of learning and of education; they must see how education connects them to the world beyond the school gates.

Educators and education are, in my opinion, the most important factors in the success of any civilised and democratic society and we must take pride in that and confidence in our ability to walk beyond the walls ourselves so that we can be the catalysts of a better, more connected and coherent future for our students.

4
Efficiency is not enough

'Nothing is less productive than to make more efficient what should not be done at all.'

Peter Drucker (1992)

In February 2013, I met the co-founder of Apple, Steve 'Woz' Wozniak, the technical genius behind their original computers. I got the chance to speak to him, at length, about education, something he is passionate about. His wife is a former teacher and he himself taught for some time after leaving Apple in the late 1980s. A few things he spoke about really stuck with me. The first was his concern that when we talk about education at the highest levels, we spend far too long debating *what should be taught*, focusing on how we make the system increasingly efficient rather than how we encourage the ability for people to learn so that they are able to continuously change and develop. His point was that we have moved beyond a world where routine cognition rules to one where innovation is the key. The idea of focusing on the efficiency of education rather than the future of it had, in his opinion, led to a closed loop that was not moving students forward but inhibiting their potential. This is not a view that is entirely unique. The OECD have on many occasions cited similar thinking, based on their findings. They are currently expanding their research and exploration of education policy to support that growing view with reports into collaborative problem-solving and social and emotional skills.

Woz's point was not only based on his own teaching experience but also, perhaps more pertinently, on his experience of building Apple with Steve Jobs. Together they could see the future of their industries, and where many companies had begun to stand still, obsessed with incremental changes based on efficiencies that protected their position and their bottom line, Apple knew the future lay in constant innovation and not responding to trends but creating them. To do that, they consciously built a team of people who didn't need managing but could, through great leadership and clarity of vision, work ahead of the curve.

'Innovation distinguishes between a leader and a follower.'

Steve Jobs (as quoted in Gallo, 2010)

Jobs and Wozniak were clear therefore that in order to develop innovative outcomes, you needed an innovative workforce.

In this chapter, I want to explore how we build capacity to teach our children to be innovative, in particular how we create innovative cultures and capacity in ourselves, our staff and our institutions. I want to explore what we need to think about and to act upon in order to ensure that we are capable of working beyond just the efficient.

As I write this chapter, the entire concept of the 'innovation' in public–private partnerships is being interrogated after the collapse of one of the UK government's major public infrastructure and service providers. What is being said over and over again is that there has been so much pressure to deliver results and so little time to innovate, in order to find more cost-effective and creative solutions, that delivery has gone backwards, now working hopelessly behind the times. It's an interesting challenge and one that is familiar throughout the world and across services and businesses. It is particularly resonant in our schools, of course, where for decades we have been talking about innovation and creativity, about the importance of it for our students and for our curriculum, but we are always held back by the narrow focus on specific outcomes. It's a case of efficiency diminishing the chances of innovation: 'Make more of the same; we don't have time to risk different.'

Eric Schmidt, the recently retired Executive Chairman of Google has said on many occasions that his greatest challenge was ensuring that the company maintained its confidence in itself and therefore its own ability to drive forward rather than, once successful, investing too much time and energy in protecting its position, obsessing about what others were doing and, as a result, becoming reactive and eventually obsolete.

In education we have a hugely difficult moral and practical challenge. We must ensure that schooling helps to prepare our children with all that they need to meet the challenges of their future; we must also provide the right for children to experience, enjoy and be stimulated by learning for its sheer pleasure, intellectual and experiential challenge. This need for innovation has always been there, but it has become more acute over the last 50 years given the rate at which the world is turning and evolving. We must also, however, ensure that, whilst shaping a system that achieves all of that, we are clear that we don't experiment and innovate to the detriment of the current generation of students; there can be no prototype generation, where things were tried and failed in order to make it right for the following cohort.

There is a fear, I think, that terms such as innovation and creativity 'water down' the gravity or importance of education. They have become terms used almost as accusations in the 'war' I talked about in Chapter 1. We have to find a way to move on from that. It is worth remembering that innovation is not irresponsible or reckless if constructed and led correctly. As Steve Jobs himself once stated, 'To turn really interesting ideas and fledgling technologies into a company that can continue to innovate for years, it requires a lot of discipline.'

I also worry that we are fearful of innovation and creativity in education because there is a myth that it is somehow anarchic and that it lacks discipline but also that it is a distraction from the matter at hand. As with the struggles between public and private partnership, where the perception was that private sector organisations possessed the time, resources and capacity to innovate and therefore create greater efficiency for the taxpayer, the reality has been somewhat different. If you set targets that are limited to highly defined, fixed outcomes then inevitably all resources go into delivery; that is true on an organisational and personal level.

Since I left teaching, both of my children have come to the end of their school careers and I have to say, on a personal note, what they went through in their final few years was tough. The school they attended was brilliant at drilling them to take their exams and, as a result, their outcomes and those of their peers were very high and very stable, but both have found self-led study tough. My daughter, who has just finished university and begun her life as a teacher, found the transition into higher education a real challenge; she struggled for a long time, coming to terms with an environment that trusted her more, managed her less and therefore expected more from her independently.

I do not blame the school or the teachers, all of whom care deeply about their students and are rightly proud of the job they do. They are, however, under enormous pressure. It is a highly successful school; the community has an expectation that its academic outcomes will be high and that students will attain university places; it is a state community school and therefore has a mixed and challenging catchment area. I know that the school would love to explore a more innovative and three-dimensional approach, but it is, given the pressure and its highly limited resources, focused on efficiency.

I feel that this is one small example of the wider problem. There is obviously a raging debate about what constitutes effective education in the modern world and we will return to that later but behind that is the delicate balancing act between the benefits and risks of efficiency versus innovation. Our children only get one shot and we cannot get it wrong for them. It is why, particularly over the last few years, I keep lurching from one position to another, constantly challenging my own viewpoints.

Let's take the challenge of the continued importance of formal qualifications, qualifications that are universally seen as a differentiating marker for students and their future lives. In 2013, the OECD report 'Skills Outlook' highlighted that one of its warnings was that if we spend too long focusing on preparing students to take the exams that lead to qualifications, we miss teaching the skills and behaviours our kids will need to be best placed in the global workforce. Why? Because systems obsessed with the acquisition of qualifications naturally focus on preparing students to take the tests at the expense of the wider skill set they will actually need in their adult lives, creating a conflict between learning and test preparation, innovation and efficiency. However, qualifications and good exam results still broaden a young person's opportunity and are currently the most potent levers for social equity and opportunity. They matter!

Governments find themselves in a tough place really; in the democratic world, they are accountable largely for their short-term actions: their efficiency. Are they spending the taxpayers' money to best effect? Are the taxpayers receiving value for money and the best return? In education, the traditional measure in schools is examinations and qualifications. This means that governments have a democratic cycle to influence those outcomes and therefore its key lever has to be efficiency; it almost doesn't have time to innovate. There are also, of course, ideological views related to policy, which, again, I will come to later.

Through the work I've done on change and sustainable development over the last few years, I have one point of clarity. Change of culture, of practice, cannot happen overnight; innovation that is responsible, considered, disciplined, sustainable and balanced requires time spent on developing capacity, context and confidence first and this alone takes time – years, not days or months. Similarly, most change in most organisations, and this is certainly true in education, is mostly reactive and not proactive. This is often exhausting and dispiriting, which can lead to a feeling of a lack of control and therefore stress. It also leads to cynicism. Reactive responses are not conducive to effective innovation because, at best, innovation becomes tokenistic, sporadic and often nothing more than short-term novelty. We have seen endless examples of this in education. Too much of what we have experienced over the last few years has been viewed as gimmicks or silver bullets, often rightly, but sometimes great ideas, powerful starting points, have been cast in the same mould and therefore ditched.

Government policy really hasn't helped; endless tinkering with the levers they control is all really about high-level systems and structures that have not only divided opinion but also added to the workload and the exhaustion of continuous reactive change. We must remember that most of any government's vision is short-term and therefore highly efficiency-based. They have not found the right balance; it's tough.

Education needs to be so much more than efficient.

'In times of change, learners inherit the earth, while the learned find themselves beautifully equipped to deal with a world that no longer exists.'

Eric Hoffer

In many organisations and fields of work, profit is the bottom line; it has to be. Not only does it pay people's wages, contribute to taxation (usually) and drive economies but it also provides the resource for research and development, marketing and innovation. Most companies are constantly performing a balancing act on a spreadsheet that defines how solvent the business is and how well it can fulfil its responsibilities. Productivity is therefore one of the defining factors in a business's success or failure: more product, more sales, more money, more profit. The difference though is that in education and indeed in public health care, there is no product and people are more than customers. Most companies will try to manage variables in order to reduce risk, whether that's the volatility of markets, regulation or competition. If you create a solid process, a rigorous system, you can minimise the impact of those variables but often at the expense of keeping ahead of your market.

When the variables are almost always human, that is even harder. Education and health care cannot be run that way; the risk is even higher. In 2017 the World Health Organization, as they do every year, had to decide which strain of flu they thought would be the most significant globally. They used all the data and scientific knowhow at their disposal but tragically they got it wrong. People were vaccinated against the wrong strain and that led to the largest number of serious infections and even deaths in recent history. People are organic and unpredictable; it's partly why we have become the dominant species on earth – for good and bad.

A few years ago, I had the opportunity to work with the legal and financial teams of one of the world's largest technology businesses, a company that has been one of the most significant in the digital age and also one of the longest serving. Each year, it invests approximately 15 per cent of revenue, billions and billions of dollars, into research and development. Its tech and innovation teams are working on some truly staggering innovations, but the business is struggling because all of the innovation is happening at product level, not in the way the company makes money (through contracts, billing and licensing), and this is the delivery arm, where outcomes are defined. The legal and finance teams were largely left untouched and asked to focus on maintaining the structures and systems they had developed over the previous 40 years, namely to focus on certainty. The business engine of the company felt that the structure and system of delivery had to remain unchanged in order to minimise the risk to the bottom line. As a result, new competitors had come along and not only developed innovative products and services but also changed the way the market ran financially and legally, offering new thinking and business delivery models, like subscription and pay as you go. The market and the customer had moved on, but the company had failed to balance its strategy across all arms of the business. As a result, it is in trouble and is now investing too much of its time and money catching up; it has found itself in a vicious cycle.

With health care, it appears that there has been a similar problem; there has not been enough investment of time or money in innovation at the delivery level and as a result people, patients, are suffering, despite massive strides in treatments and medical science. Underlining that, innovation has to be a constant through an organisation, not just in one element of it. If innovation isn't the cultural norm, it will not work; you cannot pay lip service to it by letting it happen in safe isolation. So, innovation has to exist in structures as well as in processes. It is also possible to say that in health care, too much time and focus has gone into cure rather than prevention and, as a result, an aging population, who had less health education than is now available, are stretching the system further than ever.

Maybe, therefore, the three key issues are:

- People and their environments are organic and unpredictable.
- If you focus on reacting, your resource is spent in catching up rather than moving forward.
- You have to balance innovation and development across product and structure.

I think that you can apply the same criteria to education: the challenge is in finding the balance between the structural and the process. Like health care and the tech company I described, policy has focused too much on the *efficiency* of the structural, the delivery element, despite the innovation and new thinking around teaching and learning itself. Despite the fact that innovations in teaching and learning have moved on dramatically over the last few decades (we know more about the brain, about behaviours and about the power of technology and human development than we ever have), policy has kept us focused on structures of delivery and the same traditional outcomes based on fixed data. It is easy to understand why. To lock down structures and systems means that there is less risk to children; after all, the success criteria haven't changed too much and therefore if we focus on efficiency of delivery, we will be all right. There is inherently less risk in trying to do what we have always done more efficiently. So, we have played with who runs our schools and colleges, how they are funded and what they look like. We have focused on delivering more of the same but to a more efficient degree (more higher scores, grades and qualifications), at the expense of embracing innovation, allowing it to permeate through the systems and structures so that we can change the entire process of education and allow it to truly effect change.

That is not to say that there hasn't been some stunning innovation in education; there has, often in developing countries like Colombia and Mexico, the geographical equivalents of the tech start up and places hungry for success, less tied by the pressures of tradition and with a vision built on development in the modern world. There have been pockets of exciting developments in practice in schools around the world and, of course, the impact of technology has already been immense, particularly in expanding access to an education for millions globally. I would ask, however, how much of that innovation has really led to education transformation and how much of it is still seen as disruptive and not mainstream? How much innovation has been diluted in an effort to fit within existing systems and structures rather than to catalyse their transformation?

When I look at the last ten years in particular, I have seen so many countries, especially in more established mass education environments such as the UK, US and Sweden, spend most of their time, effort and resources on how to make the existing system work more efficiently, including how technology has been used. These countries have focused on the systems and structures around managing schools and colleges. We have become increasingly obsessed at a policy level with 'league tables' published in the PISA reports produced by the OECD and other global academic outcomes data. Too many countries have then simply reacted to that with policy decisions that are designed to respond to that information in an effort to climb up the tables.

So, like the tech firm and health care, we have largely lost sight of the innovations in development in terms of product, in favour of the security we find in systems and structures. If we go back to the three earlier points:

- Have we, in an effort to drive progress, standardised too heavily and, to an extent, dehumanised a highly personal and human experience?
- Have we focused too much time and resources on reacting to historic outcomes rather than innovating and then finding ways to measure new ones? Have we let ourselves become obsessed with the wrong things, distracting us from our own ability to innovate and develop?
- Have we spent too long managing and developing the predictable and easy to control (the structures), rather than promoting innovation and real research and development?

I have to confess, I have seen so much education innovation packaged and sold in a way that preaches greater efficiency rather than as a significant catalyst for change.

To an extent, many countries are still obsessed with regions of China and their educational performance, similarly South Korea and Singapore, but if we reflect for a moment, China's education system is tied into its economic development, and although its GDP is still higher than most, around seven per cent in 2017/18, it has fallen steadily over the last few years from around 11 per cent. It has recognised that an education system built on technical efficiency and routine cognition now needs dramatic change. As a nation, China knows that it has to move on from its position as the world's most efficient factory if it is to maintain its economic growth; it needs to focus more on innovation and entrepreneurship and therefore it needs to evolve its education system to reflect that. The same debate is being had across the Asian powerhouses. They are investing huge time and effort in moving away from systems built simply on academic and technical rigour, in order to find ways to encourage and promote more creativity and innovation. They have been looking at ways to reduce the pressure on students by limiting homework and encouraging less after-school tuition and cramming. They are looking to expand their curriculum and offer to enhance experiences and opportunities that don't just focus on tests and exams. They are beginning to realise that the new economy cannot be built on the old industrial model and that economic and technological growth mean that jobs and careers need to change. People need broader skill sets and experiences and have a changing level of expectation in life.

There is more than one path

Before we go any further I want to make something clear. I believe that university and a higher education should be a universal right; all children, everywhere, should have access to a tertiary education. I actually, in my most ideological position, believe that we should, as a human right, have access to education for the entire duration of our lives. I am not anti-academia or intellectualism. I went to university and benefitted beyond measure; it's where I met my wife and found a home and a career as an educator. I have encouraged both of my children to do the same and have, along with my wife and family, supported them and their schools to ensure that they achieve, so that they have had that choice. I do, however, worry that as part of our drive to make what we do work better, we continue to make the mistake of thinking that a university education should be everyone's gold standard and that, for many, a university education today is solely about the qualification at the end of it. I want to break this down a little bit.

Firstly, for some, university is an important step in their development; as I've said, it was for me. I went to university not really sure about what I wanted to be or do; my degree was a bit of a catch-all, combined studies course, which did its job because before the end I had decided that I wanted to teach and so went on and did a postgraduate teaching qualification. A couple of thoughts though: firstly, my degree was free and at no cost to me or my family in terms of debt or taxation; secondly, it was the woman who is now my wife, whom I met during the social aspect of our university career, who actually inspired me to think about the idea of teaching – it was not my degree course.

I have spoken to a number of university vice-chancellors over the last few years and many share the same concern. Firstly, a number of students attending university really shouldn't be; it is the wrong place for them. Some are, at best, studying the wrong courses, because they were told that it would be the best for their future rather than because it was their passion. What I think is more of a concern, however, is the number of committed students who in growing numbers aren't interested in university life but just want their qualification as quickly as possible and, as a result, miss out on so much of the human development university offers. All of this is a little sad but also very worrying. Increasingly, a university education is costing students and their loved ones more and more money, which is creating high levels of stress and anxiety amongst many.

The idea of expanding university places and providing opportunity for all has gained traction over the last 20 years or so, in response to the growth of the high skills economy. The process, in the UK at least, began back in 1963 with the publication of 'The Robbins Report' (Committee on Higher Education, 1963), which first set out the ageless principle that all those who could benefit from a university education should be able to do so. The question, though, is have we gone too far? Yes, the average graduate job pays more than a job not requiring a degree but there are fewer and fewer of those jobs and more and more graduates. In 2016 it was estimated that as many as one in three graduates could not find graduate-level employment (Viña, 2016). Now I am aware that some may not have wanted one but that is still a worrying statistic, especially when you think of the debt those former students are carrying.

There are, even now, some major graduate employers who are questioning whether a degree is any longer a real seal of quality. In some professions there is a clear and growing belief that the technical skills taught on some courses, in preparation for some careers, can now be taught in-house, to the right candidates, in a matter of weeks. What is a constant is the concern that new employees, graduate or not, are lacking in many of the skills employers are now demanding from a modern workforce. This is something I will explore in more detail in Chapter 5.

There can be absolutely no argument that an educated and skilled population has a far greater chance of success than one that is less so, but I worry that we are simply ignoring the development of the real knowledge and skills our children need at the expense of tests and qualifications – the easiest way to measure efficiency. We must be braver in accepting that the skills and knowledge children need have evolved as the world around us has, and that means we must look beyond the systems, structures and pathways that have always appeared to work for us. We need to ensure that the definition of a university education as the best route to certainty is challenged. Education can no longer be about preparing people for certainty; it must be focused more on preparing people to thrive in uncertainty. A focus on efficiency and the 'best routes' has been highly successful in the past, but they are now hampering the potential innovation needed to lay the best routes for the future.

I have great optimism for the future, however, because I have definitely seen a desire from educators themselves to move away from the silver-bullet mentality that dominated so much of the 1990s and early 2000s, towards a real commitment to share practice and develop thinking. All I ask though is that we audit carefully whether we spend enough time in those discussions and during that action-based research looking beyond how we make the existing system work more efficiently.

Of course we need to develop systems that have equity of opportunity for all but that cannot be by simply improving what we already have. We have to ask bigger and more challenging questions of ourselves and of the society around us. After all, if our students are to look back on their education with both fondness and pride, it will have to have helped them achieve something in their future.

A university education, for example, should not just be seen as another hurdle on the journey that is a means to an end. It should be a choice for its value to that student and their lives in the present, as well as the future, and it should be available for those who love learning in the kind of environment a university provides, but we also need to look bigger and wider – to expanding other forms of tertiary education and on-the-job training, such as apprenticeships. As schools we must have the vision, courage and leadership to help explain, celebrate and find those right routes for our wonderfully unique students.

The human race has not evolved and developed through history because of a focus on efficiency; it has evolved because of our natural-born curiosity and our desire to learn, to challenge, to innovate and to be better. Efficiency provides a great sense of stability and confidence in the short term but growth comes from something much bigger and something far more akin to the human spirit. It comes from our eternal pursuit of learning.

5
Skills and knowledge

'It is possible to fly without motors, but not without knowledge and skill.'

Wilbur Wright (1900)

Before you flip to the next chapter in despair that I'm about to launch into a polarising, 'progressives' versus 'traditionalists' rant about whether it is skills or knowledge that should drive education, please be assured that I am not. I find the debate as tiresome and as distracting as most of the people engaged in the real, meaningful discussions about the future and current directions for education.

The arguments are well rehearsed and, for me, largely semantic. I worry a little that some confuse the term *knowledge* with *a fact*. For the record, the *Oxford Dictionary of English* (2010) defines knowledge as: 'Facts, information and skills acquired through experience or education.' It goes on to identify that the word 'skill' is derived from the old English word 'scele', meaning knowledge, and the old Norse word 'skil', also meaning knowledge or discernment. I have seen people try endlessly to justify the difference and why one is more important than the other. I have to confess that I have probably been guilty of doing so in my time. It now seems extraordinary to me that people have spent so much energy on this debate, rather than thinking about teaching, learning and developing our children for the future. We appear to have wasted so much time trying to argue that skills are more important than knowledge or vice versa that it has created real division, mostly amongst people who aren't in our classrooms working with our children, but it is distracting and has been confusing for many.

In the world beyond education there is no discourse about the importance of one over the other; there is no need. People understand that knowledge and the ability to be knowledgeable depend on the ability to utilise what you know to solve problems, and to develop thinking, strategy and solutions, whether you are a scientist, an artist, a financier, a technologist or an athlete. What defines successful people is not simply what they know but how they use it. All lawyers 'know' the law but the really successful ones have the skill to use it to substantiate their arguments. Crucially the definition above from the dictionary perhaps best explains the marriage we need: facts, information *and* skills.

It strikes me that the problem actually is that we are stuck in a loop that is similar to that of 'the chicken or the egg'. Do skills feed facts or do facts feed skills? Does it matter? To demonstrate knowledge you need both. I fear that it is a loop that too many policy makers have found themselves trapped in.

The argument that our children need to be first taught the basics is one that few can argue with; what seems to be open to conjecture is what we mean by the basics. In some ways, for me, it comes down to trust and actually whether we trust our human instincts to be curious and our born desire to learn.

Do we need children to become literate and numerate? Of course we do; they are vital skills that enable our kids to access so much that will help to develop their knowledge. What most of us realise is that knowing that Queen Victoria ascended the British throne on 20 June 1837 is not knowledge; rather, it is a simple fact. Knowing that fact will define neither our success nor our ability to succeed, in the same way that not knowing that fact will not prohibit our life chances. Being able to understand the impact of the Victorian age on us and being able to process why that impact was so profound across so many fields (science, engineering, travel or the arts) is of far greater importance. How we process facts and use them is what learning is all about; how we make them relevant and stimulating to students is perhaps where we should be putting our energy as teachers.

I often get asked if I think that technology will replace the teacher and whether I think that is a good thing. If teaching is no more than the acquisition of facts, then I would argue teachers are already obsolete, not just because of technology but because anyone can share facts. To inspire a thirst for knowledge and a desire to learn, however, is a human experience and one that technology cannot replicate – not yet at least. Technology is a wonderful catalyst and also a brilliant vehicle of communication and of democratising information, but it is not able to model the wonderfully human traits that define us. TED Talks are not brilliant, provocative and inspirational because of the technology used to broadcast them. The technology makes them accessible but the way we feel about them is entirely down to the people presenting them. So it is there that I want to focus: on the 'presenter', the teacher.

Great teachers are great leaders; they inspire others to strive, to develop and to achieve. They take information, often complex, and facts, often sterile, and they make them live; they make them matter so that they become tools in the box of a student as they develop their knowledge and understanding of the world.

I am going to take for granted that teachers have high subject understanding and knowledge themselves and I want to use this chapter to look at the skills that help us define great teaching and teachers. It is the special marriage of the two that helps us to ensure that learning lives for our students. If we want to develop our students' abilities so that they can be innovative, abundantly curious, collaborative and capable of solving complex problems, then we, as teachers, need to master the same skills. I don't want to go over old ground, so I want to share some of the insights that I have learnt from fields outside of the classroom that I believe correlate back in it and help to underline how our best teachers are already prominent experts in the fields of human development and leadership, teaching and learning.

In the opening chapter, I mentioned Google's research into great leadership and management, Project Oxygen, which was particularly focused on identifying great coaching and core human leadership skills. I can't help but think that some of these characteristics have huge resonance for us as educators.

It should be a given that great coaches, like great teachers, are knowledgeable. They know the content and routines of their job, but more significantly, they know the processes, skills and techniques that contribute to success. It is skill combined with knowledge that creates success. The better the coach understands these two elements, the better they can help the athlete to modify, change and improve their behaviour. How often have you seen highly knowledgeable, highly intelligent and academically brilliant people teach students really badly? The art is not just in what you know but in your ability to communicate it. It is, most crucially, in your deep understanding of the indivisible nature of skills and knowledge.

Be a great coach

The best coaches are highly organised. This is perhaps one of the most important traits of a great coach because it shows commitment. The same is true of the best teachers of course. By being role models and showing students our own commitment to organising their learning, it underlines to our students that we care and they then respond accordingly.

Great coaches understand that the success of their team is based on their athletes. Knowing this, they establish high levels of continuity and routine. Coaching is like an exercise programme: the more they follow the coaching schedule, the stronger their charges will become. They stick to it. This organised and committed approach tells their team that their success is important. This is exactly what teachers do when they know that the success of their cohort is based on their students.

In sports, where the quality of coaching makes the same difference to athlete performance, just as the quality of teaching does to the performance of students, the process has four key components. They focus on:

- standards
- monitoring
- analysis
- feedback.

In sport, a great coach consistently monitors an athlete's work based on what they do against a set of skill standards established in the initial training. The coach then analyses what has been done and provides feedback designed to positively modify, change and alter the athlete's behaviour. Good coaching is reliable, dependent and consistent, which is why this four-stage process is so important. I have seen many coaches falter and lose the respect both of their athletes and of their own bosses because, under pressure, they have suddenly changed tack or their own behaviour, causing stress and uncertainty, therefore adding to the problem. Inconsistency from a coach can kill a young athlete's career.

When it comes to monitoring, great coaches don't simply tell their athletes what they observed or what they 'did wrong'. Great coaches ask, 'How do you feel you went?' By doing this, the coach is allowing the athlete to participate and, in effect, coach themselves. It's a two-way dialogue, not a one-way monologue. The athlete must do the analysis. It becomes more meaningful. Ultimately, as teachers, our job is to develop the capacity for our students to become lifelong, independent learners. Bad coaching in sport leads to a high-dependency culture, which can lead to the downfall of an athlete and a team. Increasingly in elite sport, the emphasis is on the transference of responsibility for improvement to the athletes themselves. Talking to the former England rugby union coach Sir Clive Woodward, some years ago, it was clear that his entire process was designed around coaching his players so that they were able to lead themselves, something that he asserts was the difference in Sydney on the famous night in 2003 when they became champions of the world.

Great coaches are also objective with their feedback. The athlete understands that and realises it is not a personal perspective. This makes the feedback meaningful, relevant and easier to apply. It reduces the sometimes adversarial nature of difficult conversations around performance. This is one of the great skills of a good teacher too: to ensure that a student sees critical feedback as objective and developmental – that they don't feel picked on or, worse, humiliated in front of their peers.

Coaches and teachers have a tendency to deliver negative feedback about performance far more than positive; some studies suggest that this is by a ratio of 5:1. A great coach knows this and battles it. A great coach is always conscious of looking for and providing positive feedback. But more importantly, a great coach knows not to dilute the positive with the constructive. For example: 'Usain, that was a really great run, well done... But your start was weak.' A great coach gives good news and good news only. They let their athletes bathe in the praise. Or they give constructive feedback and constructive feedback only. There is no mixing of messages and hence no confusion about the message.

Whilst a great coach is process-oriented and utilises clearly defined standards to guide the analysis, they can be flexible in the manner and tone in which coaching is applied. They adjust to the personality and behaviour of the individual athlete. Analytical athletes get more structure in their feedback. Driver-type athletes get direct, no-nonsense feedback. Amiable athletes are handled with a little more sensitivity. Expressive athletes get 'banter'. This means the coach knows, really knows, their people. Great teachers are no different. In my working life as an educator, the best teachers I have ever worked with have incredibly high levels of emotional intelligence and use it skilfully to get the best out of every one of their students. They don't create one rigid style and expect the students to mould to their personality. It is important to remember that supporting elite performance cannot be delivered from on high to the masses. If we truly want every child to achieve their potential, then we need to understand and support each individual accordingly.

I have spent years trying to understand why most people resist change, even if the change is for the good. Changing and modifying behaviour takes time and effort. Some adjust quickly, some don't. A good coach is aware of that and they're patient. Athletes, like students, will make mistakes, sometimes repeatedly. A good coach is tolerant of mistakes. It may mean a little extra coaching and a little more time in training, but often that's what is necessary for success. So they hunker down and get the job done. For us, as educators, it is vital that we find ways to temper the standardised cultures that put so much pressure on us and our students to be able to all cross the line together simply because cohorts were all born in the same year and in the same geographical area.

A great coach knows when to be tough. This means identifying athletes who consistently under-perform and putting them on a performance programme. It means sticking to, creating and communicating clear expectations, putting the athlete on a plan and keeping them on task. It means regular and frequent follow-up. It means not allowing excuses and it means not extending deadline after deadline. There is always a need for tough love. Great teachers are not soft touches because they care or because they take time to really understand each of their students. Great teachers are tough and demanding; they set high standards and accept no excuses. Clarity and consistency are the keys here.

Empower, don't micro-manage

Trust is core to the successful performance of any team, organisation or classroom. If we don't trust our people then we have a tendency to over-manage them, creating a dependency culture. A lack of trust also develops a culture where people, at best, perform to expectation and never beyond it. They also have the excuse to blame others – their manager, coach or teacher – for their underperformance. Over the last few years, empowerment has become a sneered-at term, often dismissed as 'soft, woolly, liberal language', used by 'happy, clappy people'. I have heard people tell me that it gets in the way of performance and achievement. Tell that to Google! If you create a genuine culture of empowerment, the pressure actually increases on the individual, because it transfers primary responsibility to the individual themselves. The spotlight falls on them.

I have witnessed really interesting and sometimes unexpected reactions to groups who are given more freedom and empowerment, usually too quickly, after years of hyper-control and management. Many become scared and hanker after the protection of being able to blame managers and people further up the hierarchical food chain; the spotlight is far too bright after years of living in the shadows. Many of us are simply not trained and raised to live in the spotlight of accountability and that is where empowered people, teams and organisations have to stand.

As educators we have perhaps been affected most by a long-term culture of over-management and control, which has, for many, been felt as a culture of mistrust and an undermining of professionalism. There have been opportunities over the last 30 years for more constructive, open and professional dialogues that could lead to a great sense of empowerment, both for the profession and, most importantly, for our students, but they are often too short lived. When I had the honour of being appointed headteacher at Grange Primary School in 2001, the fear, lack of confidence and low morale amongst the whole school community, which had been created by a culture of over-management, was stifling; it had actually created a sort of developmental paralysis. The secret behind what happened during the next seven years at Grange was all built on a hard-won reframing of culture, built on empowerment not control and that went for the students too. As I mentioned earlier, when talking about my daughter's experience, if we over-manage our children, they may succeed on paper but we risk damaging their own self-management skills for later in life. I will talk about the leadership aspects of that in Chapter 9 but for now, I want to focus on the skills and behaviours needed to develop that culture in our classrooms with our students.

Our students must feel included, not as the passive receivers of a culture but as active participants. It is vital to share information with students; it is important because it not only helps to build trust but it also gives students important information that will allow them to make the best possible decisions and not rely on you to do so for them. The following points highlight some of the strategies we can use to audit our own behaviours in order to create a culture of real and supported empowerment.

- **Create clear goals and objectives:** Be clear and consistent with your vision, goals, objectives and roles. This will help create the framework necessary to guide students to make empowered decisions.
- **Teach that it's okay to make mistakes:** If you empower students to make decisions then you have to be willing to allow them to make mistakes and learn from those mistakes. Berating a student who tried something new will only serve to keep others from trying new things.
- **Create an environment that celebrates both successes and failures:** Don't just celebrate the successes; celebrate students who took a risk and maybe didn't obtain the results intended but learned valuable lessons. Share in your own successes and failures; if a lesson works, celebrate it, and if it doesn't, admit it to your students.

- **Support a learning environment:** This is an ongoing process where classes and cohorts look at various situations and discuss them together to determine how they might handle things differently in the future to achieve a different result. This is really what our lives and our learning are all about – learning new things as we age, by analysing the things we've done in the past.
- **Let classes take greater responsibility:** This occurs by slowly and carefully transferring controls from teacher to student. This can be a very scary and difficult process, which takes time, training and a lot of persistence. Moving from dependency to high levels of autonomy requires a significant cultural shift for some. It cannot be implemented like a new structure; it is something that you must be committed to working towards over time.

Express real interest in the individual

Make sure you show a true interest in each individual student and in their successes and personal wellbeing. This, of course, is not news to good teachers but it is something that we can all be reminded of from time to time, particularly when the overriding pressure on us is to drive levels of cohort-focused, standardised performance. Teachers in Early Years settings use the strategy as core to their practice but the higher up the education system we go, the more external accountability teachers feel scrutinised by and the harder it becomes to maintain that focus, especially in secondary education where teachers may only see students once or twice a week. Some key things to think about are:

- **Show you care:** In environments where students often feel defined by their age or ability, make sure that you show that you genuinely care more for the student than just about what the student offers you in terms of performance. They won't necessarily be the greatest asset to the stats, but they could be a fantastic individual. Some teachers, under pressure, can view their students as assets, as percentages for their targets. They therefore relate to students in terms of 'what they do for my scores'. It's not beneficial. Value is communicated when you genuinely care for people as human beings and not as elements that measure your performance.
- **Always give feedback:** As a teacher or a leader, your constructive feedback is a vital component for an individual to feel valued. Most followers are desperate for validation and they want to be recognised for their contribution. They'll follow, work and give their heart if they feel like they're following someone who cares enough about them to give them feedback about their contribution. When you take the time to give specific feedback, you are adding to their personal sense of value. I am not talking about written feedback here or even formal feedback, but tapping into what drives and motivates individual students and making a point of communicating with them in that way.

- **Appreciate your students – all of them!** This should go without saying, and unfortunately, many times it does. There are teachers who will say, 'She is a great kid.' Really? When was the last time you told her? It ought to be often! The challenge in a busy classroom is that the kids who are great are often the ones who get their heads down and get on and can, to an extent, become invisible; don't let them. It is a hugely important skill as an educator to keep all of your students in focus and to know that you have spent time nurturing all of them.

Be a good communicator and listen

It was Larry King, the legendary American talk show host, who once famously said, 'Nothing I say this day will teach me anything, so if I am going to learn, I must do it by listening.' I have often said that when reflecting back on my teaching career, I realise my students taught me as much as I taught them – whether it was about their many and varied interests and hobbies (pigeon racing, for example) or most powerfully about courage and overcoming adversity. We have all worked with young people who come from the most challenging of circumstances and some who fight to overcome serious illness or disability; they are inspirations, all.

In the intensity of the classroom it is vital to remember that great teachers don't tell, they communicate. I have seen brilliantly knowledgeable people flounder with students numerous times, because they simply talk at their audience, believing that the content itself should be both interesting and important enough. I think that one of the key rules of communication is to remember that most of the time, people don't care about what you're saying unless you're saying something they find valuable on a personal level. There has to be a context.

Good communicators establish a personal connection by focusing on how their message may impact the other person. For example, good communicators in the marketing industry always explain how the company's products or services will benefit the customer and their lifestyle. This gives the audience a reason to listen and remember what the marketer has said. As educators the rule is the same. As a teacher I would always challenge myself during planning to make sure that I only taught my students things that they found important. That didn't mean I didn't teach the tough stuff or the important things that were perhaps abstract; it meant that I would take time to find the point of connection. I would always try to take learning into my students' lives rather than try to make them come to mine.

As a teacher, there is a perception that we feel that we must KNOW. This is not just dangerous but also unhelpful, in that it creates a false aura that can make us appear inaccessible and daunting to our students. I have often seen young, inexperienced teachers try to blag their way through something, which is not only unhelpful for the students' learning but also undermines trust. Inaccurate information is worthless, so if you're not sure about something you're saying, admit it. Nothing strengthens the bond between teacher and student more than honesty and the fact that they can relate to you as a person and as a learner, as fallible.

For teachers, it should be a given that good communicators always ask questions. Most importantly, they question their audience to confirm that their point has been understood and they similarly welcome questions in return, always respecting and responding to a point of view or a need for clarification. Something I always try to remember is that just because I know what I am trying to say when I say it, my audience may not be hearing it the same way. Interaction is the best way to ensure continuity. There are many students who are afraid to ask for clarification for fear of offending you, but that fear is unneeded. Everyone comes from a different background, so everyone associates different words, phrases and even body language with different meanings. Create an environment where a request for clarification is genuinely welcomed. As with all things, if you model that behaviour as a teacher, your students will relax and follow your lead.

The most important but often most overlooked element of great communication is the ability to listen; this in itself is a real skill. To really listen requires actively processing the text and subtext, making every effort to understand what they're telling you. If you don't listen and then, as a result, respond inappropriately, you can make students feel unimportant and literally unheard. You are better off not asking than asking and then not really listening to what they have to say. Listening with your eyes is just as helpful as listening with your ears. By looking for non-verbal cues, you can more readily ascertain how someone is receiving your message, and then adapt accordingly. Furrowed brows, for example, can indicate that the other person is trying to understand your point, but not fully succeeding. If you notice, you can facilitate good communication by asking if there's something you can clarify. The subtleties of behaviour and body language can have profound implications on our lives and our relationships and by responding to and demonstrating the art of visual communication, we can help our students to develop not just as learners but as people.

I apologise if some of what I have highlighted here seems obvious but over my time, both as a teacher and since, I have often noticed that it is the 'basics' that are where the flaws and mistakes are found. We spend so long focusing on the detail – the content, the new ideas and big thinking – that somewhere in the layers of complexity the foundations get forgotten or taken for granted.

Occasionally, I think that policy makers and civil servants are guilty of overlooking the fact that teaching is, like it or not, an art form; it is a craft that like so many other highly skilled jobs appears deceptively easy when you are observing a real expert, but to achieve that apparent ease takes years of honing skills and then marrying them seamlessly with knowledge. There is no conflict between the development of knowledge and skills, in reality, for good educators; there never has been.

We cannot teach one in isolation or in preference to the other, not only because the art of successful teaching requires both skill and knowledge but because so does success in life. We owe it to our students to be the models as well as the teachers of those skills and behaviours. It also means that as teachers, we must never stop in our own pursuit of learning and excellence, starting and finishing with those basics: skills and knowledge.

6
Optimism

'Optimism can be relearnt.'

Marian Keyes (2017)

In 2011, I gave a speech at a university in Haarlem in the Netherlands. It was at the time of the Arab Spring. The room was filled with students and a number of lecturers. I talked a little about empowerment and the confidence I had in future generations to make the world a better place, to find solutions to the global crises that threaten our very futures: the environment, economy and socio-cohesion. At the end of what had been a lively and provocative session, one of the students, a first-year undergraduate, came up to me and offered her thanks. She went on to explain that I had been the first person from the older generation (a bit of a double-edged sword of a statement!) to recognise that her generation were going to change the world and, more directly, they were going to change the very nature of democracy.

I am an optimist; I believe that as educators and parents, we all have to be.

I do not believe in fate or the certainty of a pre-defined future. No matter what situation we find ourselves in now or predict for tomorrow, the future will be determined by the people who will lead it and that means the next generation: our children. I often wonder what our children today make of the events that surround them now: everything from polarised politics, terrorism in all its forms, the changing face of capitalism, all of it. Any of us who hang around young people will know that they are watching and forming their plans for tomorrow.

They care.

Around the same time as the speech in Haarlem, I was working with a major European lottery association who had recognised that lotteries, in the form we are used to seeing them, are a shrinking entity, partly because young people don't buy into them; young people are not driven by materialism in quite the same way that previous generations have been. They are also less drawn to the 'game of chance' that lotteries represent; their lives are far more unclear than ours were and they realise that hope cannot be pinned on something so fragile. As I'm sure you know, our children want experiences, a voice, and the ability to participate in and change the society in which they live.

I was also working with one of the world's largest news media organisations, who were looking at redefining the way in which news was broadcast and shared. They had realised that there was a real shift in the way young people consumed news and current affairs. Young people are the interactive generation and are active consumers. They are not sat in front of their televisions waiting for the 6pm or 9pm bulletin; they are across stories as they break on social media, often within seconds, and then their instinct is to be active – to support, to help, to contribute.

Our children are growing now in their activism and their belief that their voice matters. In the general election in the UK in 2017 there was a reported voter turnout amongst 18- to 24-year-olds of around 54 per cent (Ipsos MORI, 2017b) compared to around 37 per cent in 2005 (Ipsos MORI, 2005). The surge in support in the 2016 US election process for Bernie Sanders and in the UK election for Jeremy Corbyn demonstrated a new energy amongst young people and a growing confidence in the power of their voice. In the US, it has been estimated by CIRCLE (Center for Information and Research on Civic Learning and Engagement, 2016) that in the primaries and caucuses prior to the presidential run-off, Sanders won about 29 per cent more votes amongst those under the age of 30 who voted than Trump and Clinton combined.

On 14 February 2018, a crazed gunman walked into Marjory Stoneman Douglas High School in Parkland, Florida and brutally murdered 17 people and wounded 17 others. Tragically, we have seen events like this on too many occasions, occasions that are always followed by politicians dancing around the issues of gun control. This time, however, the students of the school decided to take action themselves and formed the group *Never Again MSD*. It has now been backed by the likes of George and Amal Clooney, Oprah Winfrey and Steven Spielberg. Universities across the US have signed up to the movement, including Yale, Harvard and Columbia. Many believe that this response will lead to the most important shift in thinking around gun laws and ownership in US history.

Our young people increasingly believe that they can change the world. It is clear that over the coming years, politics will need to shift in order to respond. Young people are voting now!

It is why I am so optimistic about the future of education, which has for so many generations essentially been dominated by a small group of older people, getting together to decide what younger people need to learn about in order to be successful. As teachers, many of us have known for a long time that education needs to be far more focused on the needs of the future and not so much on the preservation of the past. The term 'student voice' is not new. I first heard it used regularly in the early 1990s when student councils were being encouraged. This initiative, like so many silver bullets and new ideas, of course, had very mixed results. Some took it seriously, encouraging students to be involved by including them in real decision-making and encouraging them to raise real issues; others kept the whole thing at arm's length, allowing students to choose the colour of their toilets; and some ignored the whole thing altogether.

When you think about it, teachers themselves have had similar experiences over the years; there have been times when we have been encouraged to have a say, to co-develop and seriously contribute, and times where the whole idea has actually turned out to be a bit of a charade. I remember attending a number of meetings in Westminster with ministers and policy makers, where we would be asked for our opinion only to find that we had been completely ignored, with the government still selling the final policy as having been consulted on.

I truly believe, however, that our time is now! I don't know if there has ever been more need for optimism in society, more need for role models who can catalyse people's hopes and beliefs that they can make a difference, make a mark and succeed.

I have always believed that as teachers one of our primary objectives is to develop a sense of aspiration in our students and in our communities and similarly help our children to find a sense of value in the world. I used to speak quite a bit about encouraging our kids to dream by broadening their experiences and horizons and then, as educators, to help them transform their dreams into aspirations, to take a mere fantasy and make it tangible by helping them build a ladder, each step being something to learn or develop, so helping them move towards their aspiration: learning!

I passionately believe that as we nurture a young person's aspirations we must also help them to develop a sense of who they are in the society in which they live, and then growing wider from local, to national, to global, so that they develop a sense of place and purpose.

As I travel around the world at the moment, I sense a lack of that aspiration, purpose and value in so many people and organisations I work with. In schools there are teachers who care so deeply but feel disenfranchised, stressed and frustrated. I meet young people who have finished their formal education and find themselves struggling to find a sense of who they are and what they want to achieve.

Is the world really that bleak right now? Well, for many, yes, but the truth is that we all have to stop waiting for someone to change our circumstances for us. I do wonder sometimes whether we spend too long focusing on the obstacles and almost, perversely, celebrating the things that stop us from taking control and moving forward. I am not trying to pretend that it's easy or that a magic wand can make our world suddenly sparkle – I leave that to others – but I do think that our attitudes and behaviours can make a significant difference to how we process our problems and challenges.

Take our current predicament, for example: yes, for many, things are dark in many parts of the world, but if we look at human history, the greatest periods of development, of renaissance, have always come after difficult times. The age of enlightenment that followed the 'Dark Ages', the Renaissance of the 15th and 16th centuries, was characterised by an explosion in science, culture and politics, driven by a new generation who wanted better. As we stand here today, the invention of the grapheme, our ability to map the human genome and the technology that has the ability to lift millions of people out of poverty stand not only for our incredible potential but also for our ability to look beyond the current and see the potential of the future.

Our children, I believe, are well placed but they need our guidance and support to fulfil their potential and the chance at that next renaissance. I don't know about you but that opportunity really excites me. So where do we begin? Well, maybe with optimism. As teachers, we need to be more optimistic and pass this optimism on to our students in order to help them to celebrate the potential that the future holds and their role in it. Young people reflexively know that things aren't great right now and it must be partly our job to help them see the potential.

The traits of an optimist

Optimists express their gratitude, frequently

Optimists are able to find joy in the simplest of things, partly because they look out for them and aren't too busy ploughing on, head down, too focused on big issues. One of my earliest and fondest memories of education came when I was about seven years old. I was at a little urban infant school on the outskirts of London. It was 1976, one of the hottest recorded summers in English history. We had just come back into class after lunch and we were due to have maths. Our teacher took the register, looked out of the window, and then looked at us. She asked whether we would rather walk across to the park and listen to her read a story. It won't surprise you to know that that is exactly what we did. Thank goodness risk assessments didn't get in the way in those days. It's always amazed me really. I don't have many memories from that period of my life and certainly none that are still as vivid and as real as this one.

As we entered the park, we walked a little until we found a willow tree, a large one, well capable of shading us all from the sun. As we found our places and settled, our teacher started reading to us. I have to be honest and say I don't remember the story, but I do remember the moment. I can still feel it now: the sun warming us through the leaves that were gently swaying in the breeze, the grass tickling at my neck as I lay there, the smell of the dry earth and the foliage and the sound of my teacher's voice, soft and reassuring. I don't think that I had too many profound thoughts as a seven-year-old, but I had one then, one that has stuck with me ever since. I remember clearly thinking that life couldn't get any better; I was at peace.

Over the years, I have often walked or just sat in natural environments, as many of us do, when I have needed to relax, reflect or recharge.

Our jobs can feel so relentless at times, driven by timetables, curricula and targets, as well as, of course, by the drive in technology and change in our schools. I think it is hugely important that we remember the really simple things that can connect us and, most importantly, our students to the simple things around us. It's not dumbing down; it's raising up.

Optimists can find good in hardships, obstacles and failures

Strength and resilience have so much to do with confidence. Optimists do not have some mystic strength that sets them apart; they have the ability to know that they can overcome the challenges that face them because they have overcome them before. Every time you face a challenge and find a way past it, you gain a little more self-belief. A number of the people I work with, who struggle to overcome what appear to be simple blocks in their lives, lack the confidence they need in themselves, often borne out of a lack of experience gained through mastering adversity before. It isn't surprising that some of our most anxious pupils aren't the ones who always struggle or find study hard but those who have tended to succeed. I sometimes characterise them as the invisible kids: the ones who get their heads down, hide their feelings and soldier on but who often, if left, will eventually implode. I see the prevalence of it frequently in the young athletes I work with. Many possess incredible natural gifts that have always seen them succeed but they eventually find themselves surrounded by contemporaries who are better: faster, stronger and more agile. They are challenged for the first time and it is often not their talent that lets them down but their belief that they can overcome the challenge, something they have never had to rely on before; they lack confidence and therefore demonstrate what appears to be a lack of resilience.

We must therefore encourage our students to challenge themselves and allow them to fail.

Optimists are generous with their time and energy

Some demonstrate this behaviour in clear and tangible ways: they may help out in a homeless shelter or with a Scout group. The key, though, is that they give back. Often you will see them supporting friends through tough times when they themselves are not experiencing the very best of luck or fortune.

Teachers tend to be naturally highly altruistic; I'm not sure whether I have actually ever come across a more giving profession apart from in the health and social sector. As well as the profound sense of satisfaction such generosity of spirit encourages, it is also powerful because it helps contextualise your own life and the issues you are dealing with. You often hear about people who have had near-death experiences recalibrating everything and, as a result, living life in more positive and optimistic ways. It shouldn't take such dramatic occurrences and it's a little sad that for some it does but I guess that the key is that too many of us are predisposed to look inwards, particularly when we feel under threat or sense our own insecurity. By supporting others, it is not only a good thing for those you support but it also puts your own challenges into context. If I am ever going through lean spells in my work, which can happen given the nature of professional speaking, I get stuck into mentoring others. I find it helps and connects me back to my passion as an educator.

It is really important that as teachers, we remember to look up, breathe and recalibrate; otherwise the obstacles and problems can overwhelm us. But it is also why we must help our students to do the same; kids tend to be more naturally introspective, particularly in their teenage years, and we can help them develop a sense of personal optimism by broadening their own experiences and allowing them access to broadening their contexts.

Optimists are relentlessly curious

When we experience adversity it is so easy to climb inside ourselves, to hunker down and wait for the storm to pass, or to feel guilty that we feel bad or are struggling. It doesn't help that there are some who tell us to smile through everything and when we can't, we feel that we are letting people down. Teaching carries with it a huge weight of responsibility and part of that responsibility is, much like a performer on a stage or under a spotlight, to have to hide our moods from our students and colleagues. It's professionalism and I don't disagree, but that 'mask' needs to be loosened occasionally.

The problem is, educators always feel huge guilt and self-indulgence if they let that mask down. I have seen it often and in dear and respected colleagues, particularly senior managers, who spend so long behind the mask that they isolate themselves in an effort to protect others from their anxiety. One of the most important things about dealing with adversity is to be able to contextualise it, and to contextualise it, you need to keep exploring the world around you. People who are coping badly with adversity and stress tend to stop reading, talking and sharing; they feel lacklustre and bereft of energy. As a result, they spiral further away from others and experiences that could help them set their own in context or, more importantly, help them reframe their issues. It is vital anyway that, as educators, we remain curious and feed our love of learning and development, but we must do it to help ourselves recharge, refuel and move on.

For a previous book, I had the privilege of interviewing some pretty famous and successful people. What I found they all had in common was their relentless curiosity. In most cases, the interviews were set up to be time-limited. Often I would have no longer than half an hour, which meant that I had to be really prepared. This would have been challenging given how much I wanted to learn from them but what made it more so was the fact that, without exception, they wanted to know about me. In each case, their own hunger to learn was amazing. I remember one comment from Sir Richard Branson where he said to me that if 'you don't keep learning you end up wallowing in the past'.

Chicken Soup for the Soul was a book concept designed by two inspirational speakers in the US, Jack Canfield and Mark Victor Hansen. They would often tell inspiring stories about people they had met who had overcome adversity or achieved remarkable things. Eventually they decided to record the stories in a book and had it first published by a small health and wellness publisher in Florida named HCI, after being turned down by nearly every publisher in New York. The book and the resulting series of publications have clearly had a profound effect on people, with more than 500 million copies selling worldwide. The principle is so simple yet so profound; by being curious, we learn about others and derive hope from their stories, and hope is the foundation of optimism. As teachers, the more we share good news stories about role models, even former students, the more we can help to frame that sense of potential.

Optimists surround themselves with positive people

I think it's true to say that in teaching there is a category of colleague that we have all come across; actually, it's not unique to schools but it's an environment in which you will definitely find them. They could be described as wasp swallowers; they are people who feed off negativity. It's sad in a way, but I understand them. They are often people who feel under threat, or have low levels of self-confidence or self-esteem. They are people who actually are often the ones in the most need of help and support but they are attracted to the misery of others. I have worked with a number in my time: people who actually perpetuate other people's problems. You see them in staff rooms and meetings waiting to feed on negative energy. They are people who believe that they can only thrive by bringing others down or feeling that they are not isolated in their pessimism. As a presenter, I see it occasionally at events, where some people are looking to find reasons to dislike a speaker, a message or even the room they are in. It is almost as if they have filters that strip out the good stuff. What upsets me the most is that they are people who then exist in a self-fulfilling prophecy.

There is that old saying that you get out of life what you put in. I confess that to a great extent I believe in that. I like to think that I am an optimistic and a largely positive person; don't get me wrong, I have my moments (just ask my poor, long-suffering family), but I try to feed off the positivity of others. In the same way that if you hang around with people who are low, you end up in a hole, if you spend time with people who are upbeat, they can bring you up. A few years ago, I was working with a professional cricketer who was struggling with his form and just couldn't seem to rediscover his positivity. It turned out that at the time, having just moved to the area, he was living with a colleague who was dealing with stress and depression. As a result, the two of them, with no deliberate intent, kept each other down. After a few months, the new guy met a young woman who was an absolute ball of energy and positivity. He, of course, began to hang out more and more with her. Around that time, his form returned and he has since gone on to fulfil his early potential. In tough times it is all too easy to find people who will help us underline our suffering and anxiety. We must work harder to find people who can bring us out and into the light. As teachers, we know that life isn't and shouldn't always be easy; learning for students is tough and challenging and it needs to be, but we must make sure that they don't dwell on what isn't working or what they are struggling with.

Optimists don't listen to naysayers

Politics both fascinates and infuriates me; I often watch debates and *Question Time* on the BBC, and I'm a sucker for a campaign. I love watching the election battles across the world and particularly in the UK and US. In recent times, of course, there have been some extraordinary, historic moments – some political and social earthquakes – and when I look at why, it is clear that the successful parties or candidates have been very good at telling us how bad our lives are. That resonates with me, especially when I look at some of the discourse around both young people and education.

We are often told how bad our kids are and how flawed the education system is, usually by people who do it in order to then present their ideology as the solution. I'm often out with friends and I'll hear someone talk about the poor state of schools, about how behaviour is out of control and how our children are illiterate and innumerate. If I'm feeling brave I'll ask them whether they have children and if they do, whether their own children and their schools are as they describe. Interestingly, very rarely do they say the problem exists with their own offspring or in their education. Of course, what is happening is that they are hearing it through their own social media echo chamber or in the print and television media they subscribe to. The views are often coming from people with an agenda, people who want to bring others down, in order to control and to sell their own ideology.

As educators, we are hyper-sensitive to the negative; as teachers when we are observed or assessed, we only ever hear the negative. We only ever take to heart the one letter from an angry parent rather than the thanks of the silent majority. In my experience, naysayers feed off this; they are skilled at exerting their will and control by honing in on the fragility of our confidence and optimism. It's why bad news sells. It's why people are so attracted to politicians and spokespeople who tell us how bad our lives are and then promise to be the ones to fix it. In education there are great stories out there. There are brilliant teachers, in brilliant schools, doing inspirational things and they aren't rare; they are you! Find those people and be a part of that tribe. Similarly, make sure that you manage your students so that they spend time with different peers. Be cognisant of the chemistry in groups and pairings; don't always group by ability or mixed ability but sometimes by energy and attitude.

Optimists can forgive

This is a big one because it is so difficult sometimes. Schools and colleges are intense places; they are driven by people who are developing people and that means that emotions are always near the surface. Education is about morality and can be deeply personal. It is one of the reasons why I think that the peace I talk about in Chapter 1 is so difficult to come by. Anger cannot be a driver for the future yet it seems to be increasingly prevalent in our society. It speaks a little to the previous trait and the politics of hate. Honesty is one of the most important qualities in constructive development, and in order to be truly honest, we need to know that we exist in a place where mistakes can happen and, more importantly, can be for-given. One of the reasons that people often find public speaking so daunting is because they don't want to say the wrong thing and find themselves in the firing line, surrounded by people who won't forgive. It is why some people spend their lives trying to play safe and don't take the chances they need to in order to develop their ideas or their potential. Debate is such a constructive thing if it is neither personal nor judgemental. We can debate for hours with people we really trust or love. Why? Because we know we will be forgiven for disagreeing or challenging them. Optimism is about learning from the past but being able to move on and to focus on what is to come. We should be able to do it naturally with our students if and when they make mistakes or errors in judgement. Sometimes, of course, this is tough, particularly when emotions and frustrations run high; it's why investing in building trust and respect is so important early on. We need to do the same with our peers.

Optimists smile

I have believed in the power of fun and laughter throughout my career. In fact, when I was a headteacher, of the three defining words in our school vision statement – 'LIVING, LEARNING, LAUGHING' – the third was perhaps the most important. On a philosophical level, I have always believed that happy people are positive people and that positive people are the best learners. As I have already discussed, positive people are relaxed enough to fail and therefore confident enough to learn. I don't want to go into the science too much here but we know that happiness, even in small doses, releases serotonin, one of the hormones that contribute to the feeling of wellbeing. Studies have also shown that a smile, even if you don't feel like smiling, reduces the intensity of the body's stress response. Body language is so important in creating the environment around you and a smile is a great example.

Smiling is, of course, nuanced but more often than not, defuses a situation and sets a tone. I have often said that whilst education is an incredibly serious business, I don't understand why we have to be so serious when we are involved in it. I have often advised friends who have asked, when they are looking for schools for their children, to walk through the front door, stand in a corridor and if they haven't heard laughter in the first few minutes coming from a classroom, office or corridor, to turn around and walk away. To be able to smile, to laugh and to enjoy is the right of all of us; optimists know this and focus on making it happen for themselves and for the people around them.

There are times when we all feel low – when there seems to be no good in our lives or even in the world. Sometimes this is a temporary reaction but sometimes it is deeper and part of a real issue around our mental health. Seeing the good in the future and the potential for better is a crucial balance that we must work hard to hold on to and to nurture in each other and our students. We must support our own health and that of our community if we are to work against the epidemic of mental illness. Wellbeing is a complex and vital issue that needs to be at the heart of our lives and of education. The power of optimism is not THE solution, but it is a trait that needs to be worked at and one we as educators must take some responsibility for, not just for our own sakes but for our children's and the opportunities for their future. The next renaissance depends on it.

7
Love matters

'To every child – I dream of a world where you can laugh, dance, sing, learn, live in peace and be happy.'

Malala Yousafzai (2017)

When I was eight years old, my parents divorced. As for all children experiencing a breakdown in their parents' relationship, it was a tough time. I was quite a shy child anyway and very sensitive. I started to exhibit some of the outward signs of stress so many of us will be familiar with. I was wetting the bed at night, I developed a mild stammer and I was, for the first time, not really concentrating at school, not listening in the lessons I didn't like and not completing set work. As I look back now, I realise that it was partly the skill and passion of three teachers that helped me through those times and laid the foundations for me to come out the other side.

The first was the teacher I talked about in my TED Talk in Brazil a few years ago. His name was Mr Drew Smythe. He was an English and drama teacher who felt that acting could help with my nervous stammer as it would enable me to speak someone else's lines, without fear of expressing myself. The second teacher was Mrs Connelly, my class teacher, a Canadian with an incredible gift of empathy and understanding. When I was in her class, I felt safe and confident. Then there was Mr Turnbull, who, I have to confess, got the worst of me; he was my science teacher and I had convinced myself that I wasn't very good at science, so this was the subject that would take the brunt of my dissatisfaction and apathy. Luckily for me, Mr Turnbull was tough and uncompromising. He loved his subject and he cared deeply that each and every one of us achieved. It was as if I had two good cops and one bad one, just as they do in the movies. At the time, of course, I hated Mr T but adored the other two. All these years later and in hindsight I realise that all three made the difference.

Over the years, there has been so much fierce debate about discipline, the lack of it, the overuse of it, whether children need rules and, if so, how many. In the last few years there have been claims and counter claims about the state of discipline in schools, with blame being apportioned to parents, teachers, teacher training institutions, school leaders, the government and even technology. There have been a variety of responses – from the appointment of behaviour tsars to suggestions that we should bring the military in!

In many ways, the whole 'behaviour' or 'discipline' debate has been one of the most polarising of the arguments that have raged over the last few years. Sadly, as I have alluded to in previous chapters, those polarising debates and media headlines have, in some quarters, led to extremes in response and demands for silver bullets and quick fixes. I must confess that over the years I have been guilty of allowing emotional reflex to govern my responses to the arguments, none of which were healthy or, most importantly, of value to our children.

We need to deal with behaviour objectively.

We need to remember that our children are citizens, just as we are; they have unalienable rights, just as we do, and they deserve to be treated with the same respect and consideration that we expect. It is hugely important to remember that childhood, and indeed school, is not some form of purgatory that needs to be experienced on the way to adulthood and full citizenship; it is not a rite of passage. It is life, real and vital. In my later years in the classroom, as a school leader and then as a mentor to training teachers, I would always ask the same question: 'What was worth behaving for in your lesson today?'

Most children are not born naughty or disruptive but some become so. The majority, however, want to do the right things, in the right ways, when guided and instructed to do so. There are of course exceptions and we will come to that. For most though, the mix of Drew Smythe, Mrs Connelly and Mr Turnbull is the right recipe. We must remember that all children, as with all of us, are not the same. We are human – gloriously organic and original, one-off creations, which challengingly means that one size will not fit all. Like mixing colours on a palette, you always start with the primary pigments and work from there, and that is what great teachers do. We do our very best to ensure that all children have the basic skills and tools they will need in their ongoing studies and in life; we teach them to be literate, numerate and to have an understanding of the world. Then, we need to help each young person apply those skills and that knowledge so that they are able to develop as individuals, with their own interests, passions, aspirations and beliefs, using the primary colours to create their own painting.

People with perceived power, like teachers, can scare, threaten or bribe people with less power into doing what they want; that's relatively easy. I have seen many examples of this over the years, in schools, in offices, in factories and in sports teams. Very rarely does this work in the long term, partly because it creates the type of dependency culture I talked about in Chapter 5. In many ways, it demonstrates sloppy and poor management whereas great people managers are actually demonstrating leadership. Sustainable management requires the ability to connect with individuals and help them to discover their own sense of purpose, value and place in the greater mission. Most people want to feel loved, secure and of value. They want to know that they can actively contribute to a group, a team or their society and be trusted to do so, and that begins in school, often a child's first experience of community. Students need love. Love matters.

Do you want to be in my gang?

When I took over the headship at Grange, I wanted to create an exciting environment – one where students, teachers and our whole community wanted to be. The deal was simple; as a school, we would work hard to create a dynamic, inspiring and successful culture where everyone was trusted, valued and respected, but, in return, we expected everyone to accept the rules and expectations, starting with the staff. We wanted to create the right kind of gang, where entry was inclusive and involvement rewarding. Creating powerful cultures doesn't work bottom up; it has to work top down. For example, if you want the students to take risks, to learn from mistakes, to respect and support each other, the staff has to work that way first.

When, a few years ago, I had the chance to listen to Sir Richard Branson talk about vision, culture and brand, he explained that whenever he begins to develop a new concept, business, service or organisation, he starts with some fundamental questions, all of which relate well to the development of a culture.

Firstly, he works to ensure that he and his team have a sense of **clarity** around what it is they want to stand for, specifically what they want to stand for in the eyes of their customers. They discuss how it should feel to be a customer from the beginning of the interaction to the end. In schools, I think it is so important to remember that our primary customers are our children. I have visited a number of schools and colleges over the years who project fantastic values outwardly, to parents, governments, governing boards and inspectorates, but don't achieve the same clarity for their children. I used to be so frustrated as a teacher and then as a parent governor when conversations would be dominated by what different stakeholders wanted or expected, and so rarely were children front and centre of that conversation. The truth of course is that those other people matter, maybe more than they should, but if our children don't buy into the culture of our school and into the learning we offer, then we have no school of value. That is not to say that our schools should be defined by what our children want (that could be anarchy) but our children must always be our first consideration. That can be easier said than done, given the enormous and disproportionate pressure that other stakeholders exert, but it comes down to courage borne out of a vision and a passionate belief in purpose.

Once you have a deep and meaningful idea of purpose, vision and value then it is vital that behaviours and decisions match that clarity of purpose. **Coherence** is the goal here and that is all about behaviours. The truth about brands is that they are really difficult to build but incredibly easy to destroy, and inconsistency of behaviour can lead to a growing sense of inauthenticity, an erosion of trust and ultimately the end of a brand. As trainee teachers, one of our first and most important lessons is to remember to be authentic and consistent. There are those who believe that rules and control are wrong. Many over the years have mistakenly believed that I advocate that. I don't. I do however believe that sustained coherence and continuity are the only ways to develop sustainable and constructive cultures of discipline and behaviour. As with so many things, if we spend the majority of our time and energy being reactive, then people don't believe we are in control. If that happens, the trust in us diminishes and respect bleeds away. Great culture in an organisation is developed proactively, with an unremitting focus on people, their needs and the climate that will best ensure that they achieve. To do that, you need to ensure that the behaviours you want the world to see are first practised by people within the team. Behaviour management should be not reactive but largely proactive. You don't, for example, improve the health of the nation by prescribing more medicine; you do so by promoting a healthier culture.

If it's true that our schools are facing behaviour crises of epidemic proportions, as some would have us believe, then we need to look at ourselves first, not our kids. Their behaviours are most often the result of the surrounding culture, something that is again not just true of education but of wider society; it is why really dynamic companies are spending so much time and so many resources on internal cultural development. To paraphrase Mohandas Gandhi's famous quote, 'Be the change you want to see in the world':

'Be the behaviour you want to see in your school.'

That sentiment brings us to **leadership,** much more of which is discussed in Chapter 9, but leadership is the ultimate cultural radiator; it is the foundation on which authenticity flows. In all of the organisations I have worked with, one of the most common complaints I hear from people dissatisfied with their job is not the size of their pay packet but the inability of the leadership to articulate or to demonstrate vision in practice. First and foremost, leadership must be about symbolising the best values of an organisation and that is certainly true in a school. Whilst that leadership of course needs to be demonstrated by the headteacher and by their senior team, we need to remember that, as teachers, we are the leaders of the most important teams; in our own classrooms, we are the CEO or chair of the board. It is therefore primarily our responsibility to demonstrate the values and behaviours we expect; to be clear in the articulation of the vision we have and to be consistent in its application, we must symbolise our school's brand and, most importantly, our classroom's brand.

I would like to make it very clear that gangs and gang culture are dangerous for all of us, but in particular for our vulnerable youngsters. However, I believe that we could learn a great deal from gangs about the management of some of our young people. The primary age group of gang members ranges generally from

13 to 21 years. Many gang members don't fully understand what led them to join gangs but the themes tend to range from brotherhood to self-preservation. What is important, though, is what they offer young people: a sense of identity, protection and fellowship. I would like to consider these in more detail.

A sense of identity

Gang members perceive that they are alienated from society and that they have no real place or purpose within it. They often project themselves as warriors whose job it is to protect their 'neighbourhood' from the outside world. They therefore feel that they have a sense of place, purpose and value.

I don't propose that schools should project the warrior element or the sense of war, but a school should have a really powerful sense of itself and its purpose. A school should be a place where students feel not only valued but actively encouraged to take a lead in that projection and purpose, and feel a sense of ownership and identity, which tends to see them determined to preserve the image. I remember, many years ago, one seven-year-old telling an inspector at Grange that she went to an amazing school and she knew it was amazing because she had helped to make it so. This was a child who lived in care and had been a selective mute until she was six.

A school must feel like a place that students have some ownership of; otherwise you cannot expect them to want to take a responsibility for it. As schools we must work hard to ensure that each and every student is allowed to develop a constructive and personal sense of value and purpose, as an individual, not just as part of a collective.

Protection

Joining a gang, in a community with several gangs, offers considerable protection from violence and attack from rival gangs. One of the great biological reflexes across most living things is the sense of protection that a parent provides, and schools do that too, especially for children who come to us from vulnerable backgrounds. For so many, it is a safe haven – their only safe haven. Love matters.

We cannot expect our students to rock up and conform without working to ensure that they feel protected by us and in the school environment; we must remember how daunting and threatening school can feel. It is a place where learning occurs and, by its very nature, learning can be a very risky business; we must be confident enough to expose our weaknesses, our mistakes and our lack of knowledge. We can only do that successfully if we feel safe. The skill of a great teacher is never to seek to humiliate or underline weakness but to develop a climate where each child trusts that they will be protected through the challenging and scary times that being a pupil can bring.

Fellowship

Gang members often come from a home environment where a tight family structure is lacking. Gang activity offers that closeness, that sense of family. Schools must remember that every child, coming into every classroom every day, is different and that, on any given day, each child may well come with fluctuating emotions based on instability and a lack of support at home. The roles may have been reversed because for medical or other reasons the child has become the carer. The child may be in care or come from a fractured family, or one impacted by death, drugs, prison or social despair. There are so many factors governing a child's state of health and attitude that we cannot just 'control them'. They are not herds of wild animals or horses waiting to be civilised or broken in. We need to create climates that offer the fellowship of the functioning family. Love matters.

We must work hard, with each and every student, to make sure that they feel wanted and part of our society where, as with loving families, they can be forgiven and have a shot at redemption when they make a mistake or transgress.

As with gangs, membership is not a one-way street and the expectations of membership must be clear and require strong rules that have a consistency of application. We have to be careful though that the context comes before the obligations. Children need to see the value and joy of belonging to the school community; we need to make sure that they feel what we have to offer them. It will never be enough to talk to pupils at the outset about how being a student here will help you gain qualifications or do well academically. Whilst that may work for some, and particularly for those who come from family units that provide the values, sense of purpose and love described above, for many that is simply not in their context. Survival, love and safety come first. It is those things that draw people in and then promote a sense of loyalty. Love matters.

Many years ago, at the start of the original academy schools programme in the UK, I had a friend who had become the founding principal of one of the first academies in a port city in the south of England. Visiting this vast new academy, I remember being struck by two things: firstly the quality of the building (its sheer beauty and layout were inspiring) and secondly, and most impressive, the sense of love and respect about the place. The school was full of buzz and expectation, young people, many clearly from immigrant communities, moving with purpose and enthusiasm around the stunning spaces. It was a joy. Over a coffee in the communal cafeteria, my friend asked me what I thought and I underlined what I have said. He turned to me with a tear in his eye and said thank you. I was a little taken aback; he was a vastly experienced and quite tough school leader. It turns out that their first academic results had been published the week before and as one of the country's first academies, the media and a variety of politicians had leapt on what were, in data terms, disappointing scores. He and his team had been publicly vilified. As he explained, the academy had only been open for one full year and most of the students had come from challenging areas within the community. Many were involved with or touched by gangs and, in fact, according to the statistics at the time, the academy had more young people under notification of an Osman order than anywhere else in the UK. An Osman order is a letter sent by the police, following a court case or credible supply of information, warning someone that they are the subject of a death threat and at high risk of murder. They are sent out to people where there is not enough evidence to make an arrest but the threat is deemed real enough for the notification.

The school had in its first few terms become a safe haven, a place where young people were beginning to rebuild their lives, their confidence and their trust. It was a place where learning was clearly beginning to happen. In my eyes, it had been incredibly successful because it was a place where these vulnerable young people wanted to be. As a result, they were becoming fiercely proud of being there and were doing everything that was being asked of them and more.

I wonder sometimes if when we talk about love, and particularly in the context of children and schooling, we immediately think that the term is 'soft', 'liberal', 'irrelevant' or diverting from the real purpose of education. That worries me because if schools are, as I believe we are, *in loco parentis* (in place of the parent), then we must surely be places that are more than just buildings where we transfer knowledge and information, or prepare children for examinations or even simply just academic progress. We must realise that whilst these things are all vital, core elements of the job, they cannot be isolated or indeed successful if our children don't feel happy, safe and valued.

Good parents know or at least learn that the nurturing of a child isn't just about blind praise, cuddles and unconditional acceptance of behaviour; it's about being a role model. It's about setting expectations, providing experiences and opportunities to develop, ensuring that failure and mistakes happen and that they are okay and learned from. It is about chastising when necessary and explaining disappointment, being consistent in approach and tolerant of naivety. Most of all, it is about providing a sense of complete belonging, of safety, sanctuary and the conditions for growth and development. As parents, and therefore as teachers, our job is to help empower our young to become adult citizens in their own right, who can cope with their own dreams, aspirations, successes and failures. Humans are all fragile and vulnerable creatures who require the scaffolds needed to ensure stable development, much as new or vulnerable buildings do. All of that and a whole lot more relies on love.

I often get asked about my most challenging times as an educator and there is one I want to share now, one where I was complicit in the failure of one young man. It is something I think of most days, and will regret forever. As most of us do, I really hated failing a child, having to punish them and, as a school leader, having to execute the ultimate sanction of exclusion. I personally believed that if serious sanction was required, whilst not always avoidable or my fault, there was part of my action or behaviour that I needed to review, so that I as a teacher could learn and develop new strategies for the next time. Only once did I have to permanently exclude a pupil and that was when I was a head.

We had a reputation for accepting pupils who had been excluded from other settings, because our curriculum and approach suited most of them. As a result, we took in an eight-year-old boy who had been excluded from two previous mainstream schools for violent behaviour, not towards other children but most often in the form of uncontrollable tantrums that would sometimes lead to the destruction of property. It was only after he had started that we realised that this little boy was a drug addict. He had been on the streets since he was five, left to his own devices by a desperate single mother who had many children and no support. By the time he came to us, social services were involved but none of the children were in care, and by the time we became involved in his life he had seven younger siblings. Underneath it all, he was the most wonderfully sensitive kid, who wanted to be loved, wanted to do well and wanted to be good. Most days he would come into school, come and sit in my office and chat; he was good company. His life was more than disturbing. We later found out that he had been 'befriended' by a group of older kids, mostly teenagers. He had become a drugs runner and, in return, as well as a sense of belonging and safety, these older kids gave him drugs. Most mornings, coming into school, he was okay because he had had a fix, but by lunchtime he was, like any addict, coming down and desperate; that was when the violence and tantrums occurred. Eventually, because we knew he needed the care and attention a mainstream school couldn't offer him, because he needed to be taken away from the neighbourhood and put on a drug rehab programme in a residential facility, and also because he constituted a real and constant threat to staff and students, we had no choice but to exclude him. That day was perhaps my darkest as an educator. I knew that we were, in effect, sending him back to the streets where he was most vulnerable but I also knew that that would force the other agencies involved to take the necessary action. Thankfully they did. The last I heard, and it was some years ago now, was that he had been taken to a specialist facility for rehabilitation.

For me, this is the perfect example of what can happen to a child if we don't put love first and we narrow the purpose and responsibility of education. This child lost some of the most important years of his life and his schooling because he wasn't protected, nurtured or supported properly so that he could learn. He was unfit to achieve because we failed him.

As a child, I had been lucky. In my time of need, I had Mr Drew Smythe, Mrs Connelly and Mr Turnbull; I had attended a school where teachers and staff combined their skill and experience to provide the climate and culture I needed. They invested in me, and understood me, my challenges and my behaviours, and thanks to them, their care, attention and love, I was able to be a successful pupil and ultimately, I hope, a good person.

Love matters.

8
The chalkface

'I was a smart kid, but I hated school.'
Eminem (as quoted in Frammolino and Boucher, 2001)

In the US, there are currently 13 different types of school in the education system; they include traditional state (public) schools and traditional private schools. There are also charter schools, magnet schools, language immersion schools, private special education schools, boarding schools, parochial schools, Montessori schools, Reggio Emilia schools, religious schools, Waldorf schools and online or virtual schools.

In the UK, the Department for Education lists 11 categories: community schools, foundation or voluntary schools, academies, grammar schools, special schools, faith schools, free schools, academy schools, city technical colleges, state boarding schools and private schools.

Over the years and in many countries, I have been asked about which 'type' of school is the best. I can't answer that question because I don't think great schools are based on what we call them or how we categorise them. It is extraordinary though that so much debate is given over to what type of school provides the best education. In this chapter I am not going to talk about school types, because I honestly don't think it matters; at best I see it as a distraction and at worst as a way to create conflict and shift focus away from children and their needs.

As I mentioned earlier, I have a mantra: 'Systems and structures change nothing, people do.' You can classify a school however you like and you can waste time arguing over theoretic dogma that results in small shifts of system or structure, or you could explore what makes any school great. Not 'great' in the views of school inspectors but in the eyes of the people who really matter: the students, teachers and their communities.

If we went to a great school, or if our children did, we will always be advocates for that kind of system. Conversely, if we or someone in our family went to a bad school, the opposite is true. I went to a private school, something that, interestingly, people who don't know me judge me on all of the time. For the most part it was an incredible, privileged experience; the resources and environment were amazing and so were some of the staff. Some, however, were appalling. One teacher taught our class the wrong syllabus for our geography O-level exams and only realised four weeks before the tests. I turned out okay, I guess – not a superstar by any means but well enough, I hope, to live a life of purpose. My wife went to a state community school, as my own children did, and whilst the facilities and resources were not like mine, the quality of education certainly was – for the most part better actually. There were of course many parallels, including some great teachers and some dire ones, but my wife and children are, and I say this with the unapologetic bias of a proud father and husband, wonderful… on the whole.

When you think about it, a school is, in most instances, just a building or collection of buildings where young people go for formal learning to take place – just as offices are places where people go to do their jobs. Schools are hubs, often at the centre of a community, a gathering place in the same vein as a religious site, such as a church, a mosque, a synagogue or a gurdwara. What defines their quality is not what they are called or what category they fall under but the way they are run, the people who populate them and the quality of their offer. Of course some look more appealing, have inspiring architecture, beautiful settings and amazing décor, and whilst that can add to the impact, it will never define the long-term outcome. I have visited many gleaming and stunningly resourced schools where I would never send my own children, yet I have visited many with leaking roofs, peeling paint and wobbly furniture where I absolutely would!

Schools can only ever be as good as their people. In my opinion, schools are about the development of human beings and to do that you will always need high levels of high-quality, human interaction. So it is the humanity of a school that I want to explore. This is so much more important than what a school is called or how it is categorised.

Breaking bad

When looking for the qualities that define success, it can be really helpful to explore the qualities that define the opposite, so let's first reflect on some of the traits of a bad school.

A **lack of respect** is a common sign of a troubled school, a place where teachers aren't respected by their students; as a result classrooms are often anarchic and destructive places where high levels of noise, shouting and arguing impact massively on the ethos and climate. In these spaces, teachers are largely reactive, responding to behaviour and challenge almost constantly. They are places where informal hier-archies often dominate, with certain 'alpha' kids controlling the environment.

Respect, of course, is two way and struggling schools are commonly places where the staff don't respect the students and, as a result, they are places where teachers have low academic and behavioural expectations of their pupils. Trust forms the core of any powerful place of learning or high-functioning organisation: trust in its purest and most mutual form. The challenge to 'earn my respect' must work both ways and must be a priority. If there is low trust then there is going to be high threat, suspicion and, as a result, a lack of willingness to fully participate. This tension can show itself in a high turnover of staff, often above 25 per cent, which should be a concern in any employer. There are similarly high levels of absence, not just amongst students who are wilfully truanting or habitually 'ill' but also amongst staff, many of whom suffer from stress and anxiety, as do many of the students.

Low levels of self-confidence are prevalent in poor schools and link in to the high rates of stress and ill health. Teachers and students are just looking to 'survive the day'. As with struggling workplaces, people tend to arrive as close as they can to the start of formal working hours and leave as soon as possible at the end of the day. They are not social environments where people enjoy each other's company.

The **behaviour strategies are merely paper exercises** where order is only contained, if at all, by a thread. They are high-control environments, often more reminiscent of prisons than places of empowerment, opportunity or optimism. Students are almost seen as 'threats', needing to be negated, rather than fellow human beings hungry for inspiration.

Struggling schools tend to be **highly insular** places, behaving much in the same way as people who are under high levels of stress and pressure; they are in self-preservation mode where suspicion and paranoia are high and there is a silo mentality. These schools and their staff tend to cut themselves off both from other schools and colleagues and from their communities, especially their parents. They are also environments where staff show no real interest in their own learning or development. Low levels of trust and a sense of threat have a profound impact on any human being's capacity to learn; student or teacher, we are all basically the same.

Neither student nor teacher has any desire to be connected to the 'brand' of the school, which means that the respect given to dress code and uniform is patchy; staff can appear as unkempt as the pupils. There is also very little stability or consistency to the preparation or planning of teaching and learning; teachers don't tend to collaborate internally and the culture of self-preservation impacts directly on the quality of lessons and the continuity of practice.

As damaging is the school's **reactive instinct** towards new ideas, programmes, policies and fads. Poor schools are often places where people feel they are drowning and are desperate for a life raft. They are places that are particularly susceptible to silver bullets, the neatly packaged fad, sold to them by a slick presenter, 'expert' or 'consultant' who has promised quick and easy solutions. As a result, they lurch from one system to another, undermining trust, integrity and professionalism, which then results in a further dissolution of vision and values, a rise in scepticism, anger and stress and, tragically, the perpetuation of a vicious cycle.

I want to make it clear here that the vast majority of schools I have had the honour of visiting are not like that. Most are filled with good people, doing great work, making a real difference to the lives of their students and their communities.

Being great

So now for the good stuff and what makes a great school – an inspiring learning environment, a powerful community hub and a centre of life-changing opportunity.

I have learnt so much over the last few years about what makes a great and successful school by correlating my experiences with inspirational organisations outside of education. I have found that **leadership** is, of course, vital and so important that I want to pick it up separately in the next chapter bearing the same name. Something that both successful schools and organisations have in common, however, is a clear, authentic and shared **sense of vision and mission**. This comes from having a real understanding of the context of the community: its challenges, its identity, its culture and its history. No two schools are the same because no two communities are the same. You cannot simply impose your values, your culture or your vision on a community any more than you can on a state or a country. History is littered with lessons where one culture has tried to impose its methodology on others. It is one of the reasons why I believe that a system taken from one successful school or education jurisdiction that is dropped into another never works. Finland's success in education is as much to do with its geography, demographic, population size and, most importantly, its culture, as it is to do with what and how kids are taught in school. A sense of mission must be owned by the community and evolved by it; staff, students, parents and wider stakeholders need to know the purpose and expectations of the school and, most importantly, must sign up to them.

Clarity of shared purpose makes it far easier to establish clear and consistent goals and objectives because they have a place and a context understood by all. Everyone understands their role in the success of the school and their value to the process. Parents, for example, can't just be called upon when there is a problem with their child, or to donate hard-earned cash to subsidise the school's budget; there must be real collaboration and that doesn't come from merely agreeing to how many hours of homework a child should do or how many pages of a reading book they should plough through. The sense of purpose needs to be wide-ranging and inclusive; no stakeholder, at any stage, should feel preached to – that is not partnership.

A successful school must have a **relentless focus on teaching and learning** and that must therefore be at the heart of the mission. This too is not a one-way process. Great teachers and great schools do not say to their students, 'Sit down, shut up and accept what I am about to tell you.' Conformity is important but it is a mutual conformity and that means that students must be understood, and therefore the commitment must be to design teaching and learning that is rich in both context and experience. Learning must matter to students – and over and above the importance of tests and exams, the threat of punishment or the carrot of symbolic reward earned through compliance. Whilst the design of learning is anchored by core skills and knowledge, great teachers, like great tailors, adapt and manipulate so that the learning fits each child's unique frame; it matters because it relates to their pupils' interests and experiences whilst challenging them to look further and to explore deeper.

There is a **rigour to the curriculum** and an expectation that teachers can and do bring it to life. Curriculum is seen as far more than simply a syllabus, and every planned learning experience during the school day, including 'extra-curricular' activities, is a constituent element of the curricular offer.

Because the curriculum is contextualised and is focused on meaningful learning and development, it feels owned and that leads to a **culture where everyone wants to succeed**. As a result, staff and students do not begrudge hard work but believe in it; it's lean and there is no feeling of wasted time and effort but there is a strong desire to achieve excellence by all, for all. Good performance is always acknowledged and celebrated but again this is not fixed to one criterion but is based on an individual's personal engagement and progress.

There is no doubt that students have far higher chances of success in school when **parents are actively engaged** – where school isn't simply perceived as free child care or 'the place where I send my children to learn'. Partnership, as I have highlighted, is vital, but real engagement means an investment in parents: their skills, knowledge, expertise and interests. The untapped resources parents can offer are huge and by taking a real interest in their lives, you underline the sense of value you feel for them.

One resource that great schools exploit is something I hinted at in the previous chapter: alumni. Now I know that many perceive the idea to be the preserve of certain schools in certain communities, or even universities, but great schools, regardless of where they are or the communities they serve, have stories of success: former pupils who have gone on to achieve amazing things. These people are vital because they can reinforce the contextual link between school and the community, as well as being fantastic, inspirational, yet tangible role models for students. It is vital that schools project a sense of expectation *to* their community and ultimately *from* it. In some communities schools can be at the heart of regeneration or reinvention, but conversely bad schools can be the perpetuation or underlining of community fracture or failure.

Most of us tend to live up or down to expectation and it is why one of the most powerful traits of successful schools is their **sense of expectation**. I have worked in a couple of schools in challenging communities. In one there was an overriding culture of: 'What do you expect from them? They come from this place, after all.' Another, however, passionately believed that its pupils could lead a complete shift in the culture of their community. Great teachers, in great schools, will not allow excuses for underachievement to get in the way. That is not to say that they are unrealistic or dismissive of real challenge or adversity but they passionately believe in the potential of each and every child to find a sense of purpose, aspiration and achievement. They are relentless in their sense of belief in and for every one of their cohorts. As a result, a constant underlining of belief and opportunity leads to a community of teachers and students who work hard and with drive and ambition.

I am committed to the belief that if we, as teachers and parents, don't dream big for our kids, who will? Not through our dreams, by the way, but theirs. In both roles, I have only ever wanted my kids to be able to say, when their lives are reaching an end, that they lived lives of meaning, purpose and fulfilment – that they were largely pilots of their own journeys, not passengers on someone else's.

Developing a powerful, positive culture does not happen by accident; it takes **sustained effort and resilience**. People and organisations cannot lie to themselves. In other words, it is relatively easy to project an air of positivity and belief superficially, and when things are going well, they are easy to sustain. It is only during the tough days, the bad runs, the challenging periods that you truly come to know the strength of a place's culture and climate. Over the last few years, I have seen that most often tested in elite sports teams. Winning can sometimes paper over the cracks; the start of a new season for a sports team is usually filled with optimism: young, professional athletes, who have been training hard in preparation for the gruelling schedule ahead, are like caged lions waiting to be released. If they get an early win, which can often happen, the belief soars, but if the culture is fragile – say for example, there is a tenuous relationship between coach and key squad members or cliques in the dressing room – then like ice in a small crack in damaged tarmac, the crack can quickly develop into a chasm. Adversity is the best test of the robustness and authenticity of your culture. No school is or should be all unicorns and rainbows; as well as being an unrealistic expectation, this is also not an honest representation of life. Sports teams show how strong they really are after a defeat, and the main indicator of that strength is the togetherness, especially through the analysis of performance, which is honest, sometimes challenging, but always constructive. No one person is ever blamed but they are challenged to improve. Great teams don't just look at the weakest performer; they look at what each team member could do better to improve that performer.

Great culture in a school starts, of course, with one that is **conducive to, models and celebrates great learning**. It praises and rewards good performance and excellence publicly. Staff receive praise and reward for their own learning and development and the core of that is always for their focus on student-centred teaching. Great teaching requires great selflessness, courage and reflection. Great teachers model the very best of what we want our students to be and they should be recognised and rewarded accordingly.

Outstanding learning environments are **safe spaces**. There is a zero tolerance of violence, bullying, drugs, theft, misconduct of any kind and gangs, and not just amongst the student body! **Expectations are entirely consistent** and are conditions that the entire community agrees to – not just the students and staff but parents, carers and external visitors too. The emphasis though is not on what you can't do but on what you can. Deeply embedded in the climate is an emphasis on the positive values of the culture: respect, honesty, hard work, caring, fairness and self-discipline. It is worth again underlining that it cannot be that the culture is only relevant or expected of the students. The role models are the staff, all of the staff, not just the student-facing teachers and support teachers. Truly great schools have the courage to enforce the culture throughout the school community.

Continuity is so important to the successful development of a powerful culture and for schools working towards a constructive transformation, that it is vital to understand that cultural shift does take time and must be respected for such. Do not be disheartened if the shift appears incremental and slow; if there is real evidence of evolution there will come a point of acceleration and real success. Remember that silver bullets look great in the short term but never work for long.

Greatness can only be attained and, most importantly, sustained through a **continuous commitment to learn, develop and challenge yourself** and often the toughest challenge therefore for a successful organisation or team is to continue to develop even at the height of your success.

Sir Alex Ferguson, the legendary former manager of Manchester United, used to focus on the challenge of the following season within a day of winning a title. I remember speaking with Sir Dave Brailsford, the former head of UK Cycling, after the London 2012 Olympics, which saw the UK dominate everything that was two wheeled and peddle powered. His great concern at the time was the challenge of starting the training camps and programmes for the Rio Games in 2016. The concern was not around the work ethic, the athletes or the training staff, but that he was going to have to challenge winners, the best in the world, to change their practice in order to stay great. Why? Because he knew that the other powerful cycling nations would be innovating in order to improve, and that to stay ahead, Team GB would need to do the same.

In schools and colleges it is more important than ever that staff are given the opportunity for and are committed to challenging their own practice and processes. It doesn't have to cost huge amounts but must involve mentoring, in-house and external professional development, the delegation of tasks and responsibilities, and the expectation that everyone will participate. There must be a culture of continuous, action-based research at the heart of any learning organisation. Complacency kills performance.

Organisational excellence can only be meaningfully achieved if every member of staff takes responsibility and is prepared to be accountable for their own development. Jürgen Gröbler, another of the UK's successful Olympic coaches, used to demand of his rowers that, as well as physical skill, commitment and belief, they were capable of managing their own performance, knew what they needed, solved problems and drove their own training.

Underlining all of this is, of course, **teamwork**. I will never tire of emphasising the vital role collaboration plays in any field but particularly in education. It takes great courage to be collaborative because you need to be able to be honest and share your weaknesses, concerns and fears as well as your strengths. It is also vital to understand that by sharing your own expertise you are not just giving of your time in a one-way transaction; you will learn too. I have worked with one or two high-performing schools in my time who have been asked to collaborate with other learning communities but have resisted for fear of watering down their own performance. We should not be arrogant or naive enough to believe that we can only learn from people who are 'doing better than us'. I have said many times that I have learned more about character and overcoming adversity from some of my most challenged students than I have from other experiences in my lifetime. We all have different perspectives, some nuanced, some blatant, but all are important and have the potential to be profound. Great schools are fantastically collaborative places where teachers not only support each other but also learn from each other and solve problems together, using their unique perspectives and experiences to discover new ideas and techniques for different groups of students.

I remember in my early days as a teacher, I had a boy in my class who was causing me real problems; he was a natural leader who was disruptive and didn't want to learn what I had to teach him. I used standard punishments, more to show the rest of the class that he wasn't getting away with it than to actually alter his performance. I was really not sure what to do. Fortunately for me, my co-teacher was a wise and highly experienced teacher who was actually about to retire because she couldn't cope with the monumental changes in school at that time: the National Curriculum, external testing and inspections, for example. She was amazing, despite her own struggles. She truly understood children, and particularly the ones at our school and in our community, as she had taught there for over 30 years. She explained that the boy in question was actually lacking confidence as a learner and felt vulnerable in the classroom but that outside school she knew that he kept and trained racing pigeons and that was his passion. Apparently he was really good at it too. Acting on her advice, and in the days before detailed risk assessments, I arranged to take the class to where he kept his pigeons and asked him to tell us all about what he did and how he did it. After the visit the young lad's attitude completely changed. He became open, responsive and ready to learn. Thanks to a little wisdom, knowledge and collaboration, *we* helped that student as a learner. Successful learning environments are driven by collaboration and the trust in and of staff to take the initiative and make decisions, together. It is all about the assumption of excellence I referenced in Chapter 1 in relation to dynamic organisations such as Google.

Great schools are beacons, beacons of hope, of opportunity, of learning and of generosity. If schools are the breeding grounds of tomorrow and if tomorrow is to be bright then we must carry the torches with conviction and courage to the very hearts of our communities, no matter what kinds of school we belong to. A great learning environment is created by people: the staff and community of a school. The chalkface is the same in every school building, no matter who owns it or manages it. A great school is defined by the quality of its people and their skill, commitment and passion. It is a community that defines a school, not the name or management structure.

9
Leadership

'Leadership and learning are indispensable to each other.'

John F. Kennedy (1963)

On 6 July 2010, Her Majesty Queen Elizabeth II addressed the United Nations General Assembly for the first time since 1957. She emphasised in her speech the importance of leadership and in particular the strength and characteristics of leadership needed to deal with a changing world and to meet the challenges facing us all today. In her historic speech, she said:

> *'I know of no single formula for success, but over the years I have observed that some attributes of leadership are universal, and are often about finding ways of encouraging people to combine their efforts, their talents, their insights, their enthusiasm and their inspiration, to work together.'*

As Her Majesty highlights, there is no one way to lead, no secret formula or single model. The common truth of leadership is that it must be authentic. Leadership shows itself in so many different forms but, of the many experiences I've had over the last few years, what keeps being underlined to me, and what provides me with the greatest source of pride, is that great school leaders, people from my profession, are some of the best leaders in the world, regardless of field, industry or profile. What is incredibly clear too is that the grounding for that outstanding leadership comes out of the classroom and the very fact that great teachers must have the support of the school's leadership every day, in order to really make a difference to the lives of their students. A teacher's ability to lead their students begins with the school's leadership team and their ability not just to manage but to promote and model the cultures that allow teachers to have the confidence to express their talent and skill and, ultimately, to lead learning.

I never believed that I would or could have anything to say to people beyond education, especially to those in senior leadership positions in sectors beyond the school gates, but the things that skilled school leaders do instinctively, that so many of us take for granted and assume are just part of the job, are at the very least excellent and at times revolutionary outside of our own sector.

I have always said of leadership that the real privilege of the role is that you get the chance to serve the people who work with you and for you. The joy in great leadership, as with great teaching, is being able to empower others. Leadership is not about power or status, although sadly there are those who believe otherwise. Great leaders don't use the role for their own ends but for the betterment of their peers. Ultimately, and perhaps perversely, great leaders should be so good at what they do that they render themselves redundant.

Leadership, as with so many successful human relationships, starts with the ability to establish honesty and integrity. Trust is at the heart of any successful human connection. Leadership is no different. At its heart, leadership is not about implementing systems and structures; it's about people. If leaders are to inspire the trust necessary for any organisation to function successfully then they must be the role models, and the projection of integrity and honesty must come from them. Leaders must be the living embodiment of an organisation's vision, values and mission.

In this chapter, I want to make some of those skills, attributes and behaviours explicit so that you can celebrate the qualities of school leaders and perhaps challenge yourself to go further. What is clear about all great leaders is their instinct to listen, to reflect and to learn.

The challenge of school leadership

Schools are incredibly challenging places to lead because their entire business is about human potential. Schools are, by their nature, intimate places where emotions run high. Yes, they are high-pressured but so are most places of work. The difference is that the 'product' is people. The vast majority of employees who work in education choose to do so because of a sense of vocation. Most love helping others and want to have an impact on young people's lives. Many are passionate about their subject area and want to share that passion with others, and the vast majority care deeply about doing the best job they can. Schools are, however, complex places because they are places where ideas, intellect and a sense of higher purpose rule, which means that it is very difficult at times to be objective or detached. They are intense communities.

As with so many environments where passionate, highly skilled people congregate, there are the very human challenges of pressure, jealousy, stress, fear and self-protection. Schools are not places where people can go for some respite to a quiet office, or spend a few hours hiding in a corner, protected from interaction by a computer monitor; almost every minute of every day is about relationships. It is why trust must be at the very centre of a school and, for that, honesty and integrity have to be deeply embedded. As a school leader, the real challenge is to ensure that your behaviour models those qualities and to ensure that, despite the enormous pressures, leaders never compromise their values and core beliefs. The number one reason for employee job dissatisfaction across all sectors is where leaders are unable to articulate or act upon vision and values.

One of the most regular questions I get asked by colleagues keen to explore a future in school leadership is: 'When do I know I'm ready?'

As we know, a great deal of the anxiety of aspiring leaders is around functional knowledge: understanding budgets, health and safety, employment law and child protection, for example, and whilst important, of course, the truth is that these are things you learn about on the job. My answer relates to confidence and belief.

You are ready for leadership not only when you look at the leaders you work for and you start to see things you would want to do differently, but also when you know that you could, under the spotlight of ultimate responsibility and accountability, stand by your decisions and be eloquent enough to evidence that they are based on your vision and values. I remember when I was a deputy head, having endless constructive, but heated, conversations with the head about strategy and forward thinking. In our reflective moments, he would say to me that you don't realise how much harder it is to make a tough call when you are at the top of the accountability chain. He was right and I only realised it when I became a head myself. He has always served as a role model for me and I hope that our long-lasting friendship is actually a testament to his skill as a leader.

What it takes…

Great leaders must possess high levels of confidence and self-belief – not arrogance but a confidence that nourishes courage. The people you have the privilege of leading won't always agree with or even understand some of the decisions you have to take, but if they know that you are confident in them and are prepared to stand behind them they should support you.

Confidence is not the same thing as being an extravert. Some of the best leaders I've met are quiet, reflective and calmly assured, and that is because they have the courage of their convictions and faith in their process. Often, the loudest and most dramatic leaders are actually the ones who rely on the strength of their personality to drive a culture of cult leadership because they don't have the deep belief in their own thinking that nurtures genuine confidence. It is why they are often the leaders who don't have longevity in post and are also the people who start a role with a persuasive energy, a feel-good factor, but often end up in conflict and disappointment.

Possibly the most challenging job for a leader is to persuade others to follow, so it is crucial to remember that your behaviour is under constant scrutiny and that your position as a role model is central to your success. As teachers, for example, you cannot expect your students to take risks or bounce back from failure if you don't model that behaviour. You cannot expect students to respect you if you don't respect them. As teachers we also know that if we model a passion for learning and an enthusiasm for our jobs, then students are far more likely to model that back. As leaders, therefore, it is so important to model the behaviours we want to see in our teams. Inspiration doesn't just come from fine words or the right walk-out music after an assembly or staff meeting; it comes from the nuanced behaviours you exhibit in the daily challenges of the job. When under pressure, they will be watching you to see how you cope: can you stay calm and show constructive and positive approaches to the problem? Do they see you motivated and motivating through the dark days? Captaincy of a sports team is easy when things are going well. The mark of a great captain is their ability to lead their squad out of adversity by being the role model, by delivering their career-defining performances in those moments of real challenge. The same is true of a coach. Watching a head coach's behaviour during a football match, for example, can be really illuminating. There are some who prowl the touchline, gesticulating when things are going well but who retreat to the relative invisibility of the dugout when their team is struggling. People are far more inspired by actions than by words.

It's okay to show your passion! Leadership is not just about standing back and surveying. The people you work with and serve want to see you get your hands dirty; they want to know that you are in the trenches with them. For people to respect you, they need to know that you are human. It's something that again great teachers do instinctively. If, as a teacher, you project an air of knowing everything, of being faultless, then your students find you alien, daunting and 'not on their wavelength'; if you show emotions, reactions, behaviours and feelings, they can connect with you and then deeper trust and mutual support flourish. The same is true of leadership. When I was a teacher, I wanted to know that those leading me could inspire a class of students on a wet, cold Thursday afternoon. Authenticity is so important. Ideologues do not make great leaders; pragmatists do. Maybe that is why most real educators either don't want to engage in or are frustrated by most of the education debate I referred to in Chapter 1. They don't want to talk about it; they want to get on with it.

In the corporate sector, there appears to be two types of CEO. The first care about the sector they are working in, have a background in it and have often worked their way up through it. They tend to be authentic, knowledgeable and passionate about their work and that inspires those who work with them. The second are seen as mercenary, professional CEOs, people who move for the money, the profile and the personal challenge. They flit across sectors and industries and often spend no more than three years in a post. One of the major side effects is that they leave trails of cynicism in their wake, cultivated by short-term strategies and ideas that are often not properly implemented or embedded, that lack understanding of the unique context and are based on ideology rather than experience. This second group often talk a great game and are highly charismatic, but have a history of leaving before their veneer starts to crack. They are in it for the moment, not for the legacy.

Whilst it isn't important to be highly charismatic or a powerful orator to be a successful leader, it is vital that you are a good communicator. Linking back to confidence, you need to be able to transmit your vision and values to your team and community in clear and simple ways; endless verbose documents, PowerPoint presentations or memos won't help. People want to know how they can translate the vision into practice and how they can feed into what becomes a two-way process.

Leadership is most definitely about the art of listening as much as it is about the art of talking and, as we know, communicating is not a one-way process. Your words, though, do make a difference, especially when allied to your actions; the key is engagement, just as it is in the classroom. When you look at some of the most successful world leaders in recent times, the vast majority have been described as great listeners who have the ability to translate need into vision and vision into practice. They also all have had the ability to communicate through a precision and clarity of language. As a leader it is sometimes a challenge not to seek to over-justify your position by giving complex and detailed evidence, but to communicate it through your ability to connect to people emotionally and through context; that is where story-telling can have such power. As a speaker, I work hard to build a trust with my audience, a trust that allows me not to have to spend the hour of a speech talking in detail through my evidence, but that allows me to connect to the heart of my points via human connection and the telling of evocative stories. One of the defining moments of my headship was when we talked about turning our school into somewhere as exciting as Disney World. It created a clarity of idea and connection that then led to professional development and detail.

For all of the consensus of great leadership, there are of course times when making decisions sits firmly on your shoulders and requires you to be decisive. The intellectual challenge of working through all of the variables and auditing your own objectivity cannot be underestimated and forms a huge part of what it takes to be a leader. I have always found that successful leaders have at least one sounding board – that person or group in whom you trust, who has the confidence to challenge your thinking and help you ensure that you have the confidence in your decision to be able to stand by it and see it through. 'The buck stops with me' is high-stakes because every decision you take potentially impacts on many people: their work, their lives and their future. Whilst you have to be decisive you must not allow yourself to become isolated. When I was a head, I had Les and Pam, hugely experienced teachers and school leaders who worked with me on our leadership team, both of whom I trusted totally, not just as confidants but to challenge me. Leadership can be incredibly lonely, but it doesn't need to be. You need others in order to ensure your own objectivity at times and that, in turn, helps you to have the confidence to be decisive.

All leaders are aware of their accountability and that is certainly true in education. The pressure on school leaders has never been more intense, given the levels of scrutiny that they are under. I fear that the culture we have seen evolve over the last few years in our schools is the equivalent of living in a society that believes you are guilty until you can prove your innocence, and that is just wrong. Whatever my view on it, however, that is the culture that appears to exist and that means that the whole concept of accountability has become negative and adversarial; it has become an increasing source of stress to even the most experienced and accomplished of school leaders. It is therefore difficult to talk about the importance of the accountability of leadership as a vital part of the role.

The American businessman and magazine owner Arnold H. Glasow was reported to have said: 'A good leader takes a little more than his share of the blame, a little less than his share of the credit.' Whilst I think that this is a great sentiment and largely a fine aspiration, I think that currently, in school leadership, it's extremely difficult. Too often leaders take most or even all of the blame, because of their sense of responsibility and in order to protect their staff, whilst they selflessly take none of the credit if things go well. This isn't healthy because it leads to a dependency on leadership, which, in turn, allows staff to pass responsibility and accountability back up the line, defeating the very notion of leadership. If leadership is about empowerment and therefore the devolution of responsibility, then accountability must be shared. An excuse culture helps no one in any organisation and certainly not in a school. Leaders must be prepared to hold others to account so that they promote that idea of collegiate responsibility. One example would be that a teacher cannot simply blame behaviour issues amongst students on the leadership; they have to take responsibility and a level of accountability for it themselves. Similarly, leaders must not be shy in celebrating their own roles in success, whilst they must certainly be prepared to congratulate and highlight others. I know full well that the profile I gained when I was a head was a reflection of the incredible skill of my staff and students, but I am also comfortable with the acknowledgment that my leadership played a major part in stimulating the success that led to that profile.

The generosity of leaders must work both ways in times of success and in times of failure; as a leader, you must not allow others to pass their problems and responsibility on to you in order for them to abdicate and alleviate their own.

One of the great arts of leadership is the ability to delegate and therefore to empower. Crises most often occur in organisations when the majority of time is spent reacting to events and circumstances. Inexperienced leaders are the most at risk; wanting desperately to prove their worth and their standing, they tend to try to deal with everything and eventually they drown under the sheer volume of issues. Leaders must ensure that they have time to focus on key issues and proactive strategy. They must also have the time and space to refresh their own experiences and to stimulate their thinking. I know so many school leaders who sacrifice their own professional development first and who feel guilty about spending time outside of the school gates. As educators, we are a funny bunch; we seem to feel that it is the level of self-sacrifice that demonstrates how much we care. Whilst this is a powerful underlining of our selflessness, it isn't constructive as a leader. If we are honest, we have all been out of school for a day here or a day there and we have all seen those colleagues who are on the phone at every break, some who rush into school before their meeting and then rush back out afterwards.

Micromanagement is one of the most common destroyers of great leadership for a number of reasons. As well as diminishing time for actual leadership, it further exacerbates the culture of hierarchical dependency. Perhaps most damagingly, it undermines the trust staff feel you have in them. There is nothing worse for people than thinking that you don't think that they are capable. Part of leadership must of course be about succession planning; it is therefore vital that you give opportunities for colleagues to take on challenges, to step up and to show their potential. Of course, as a leader, you must provide colleagues with the resources and support they need to achieve their objective but you must also give them the chance to take responsibility.

One of Apple founder Steve Jobs' most reported quotes is: 'Innovation distinguishes between a leader and a follower.' (Gallo, 2010) That in some ways sums up so much of the challenge around leadership in education globally. There has been so much change in the system, so much talk and then policy, and so many new fads, that most educators are exhausted by the very term 'innovation'. Most teachers want stability. We are however trapped in a bit of a loop right now, partly, and perhaps a little controversially, because of a lack of real leadership at the top of education. The world is turning and evolving so fast; Jobs himself led part of the technological revolution that has changed everything, mainly the rate of change itself. Most schools and school leaders have been trying to manage change. It has been exhausting, reactive and somewhat dispiriting. As I highlighted in Chapter 4, most of the change has not been proactive, but to an extent focused on how we do what we have always done but more efficiently. School leaders, as with leadership in other fields, need to find the time and energy to be innovative and creative.

In my book, *Change: Learn to Love It, Learn to Lead It*, I talk about change and the need for it to feel as imperceptible as the daily growth of your own child. Sadly, for most in our schools, it doesn't feel that way and that is where leadership needs to play its part. Innovation is not something you plan on a five-year cycle or have a training day on; it is about a culture, one where ideas are encouraged, nourished, discussed and trialled. It is a culture that can only be nurtured by promoting new experiences and stimuli. Creativity must be encouraged as part of daily routine, and that takes skilled leadership and courage. This could be simple things like auditing how much time is taken in meetings for the procedural or the focus on efficiency and how much is spent on new ideas and thinking.

As schools, we should be better at modelling innovation and creativity, not in the classroom but in the staffroom, and that must be modelled through leadership.

As a school leader, I would often encourage talk in staff meetings, about books people had read, YouTube clips they'd seen or experiences they'd had outside of education, as catalysts for discussion. For example, how could you use a GoPro or a phone's video camera to demonstrate paragraphs in writing? It is worth underlining the theme of Chapter 3, 'Beyond the walls' again here: that leaders must get out more or, at the very least, meet with people in other sectors to discuss issues and challenges with the stimulus of fresh thinking, viewpoints and ideas. I honestly think that one of the most transformative conversations I had when I was a head was talking with the people development manager at an internet bank about how to create happy cultures in intense and results-focused industries. Once you have nurtured a culture of innovative and creative thinking, it is vital that you harvest the fruits of everyone's labour and the skill and challenge there is to develop capacity, perhaps through action-based research, to turn ideas and goals into reality.

The last trait of great leadership I want to highlight should perhaps be the easiest for teachers and that is empathy. This is the instinctive behaviour that I truly believe makes great teachers and school leaders special. In so many other fields, I have seen leadership rely on hierarchy and power to drive their colleagues, yet as teachers we are schooled in the power of persuasion and of truly understanding and acting upon the unique needs of our students. In this way, great teachers are already at the forefront of leadership and school leaders just need to remember to think and behave exactly the same way with staff. Just as any teacher forced to sanction a student should, when reviewing the events that led up to that sanction, review their own behaviour and actions, so a leader should be similar.

Above all, great leaders need great empathy. When England's football team won their first ever penalty shootout at a World Cup in the 2018 tournament in Russia, they did so under a manager, Gareth Southgate, who had experienced as a player the pressure of missing a penalty in a major international competition, and whose empathy with the players and situation he was managing led to preparation that emotionally readied his squad for the challenge. As school leaders we must never forget what it feels like to be a teacher and we must remember the art of great teaching as a trait of leadership. Richard Branson once told me that he turned down the chance to star in the television series *The Apprentice*, on both sides of the Atlantic, because at the end of every episode, the leader has to dismiss a candidate with the flourish, 'You're fired.' His belief as a leader was that if you actually have to fire people, and occasionally it has to happen, then you have played a significant part in that failure and it is not something to be proud of. It is my belief that everyone has a strength and it is the job of a leader to find it and to use it to bolster and develop weaknesses.

There is no one way to lead – no clear personality, behaviour or system – but there are traits. Real leadership, though, can only come from within; great leaders know themselves and are comfortable in their own skins. They have the courage to stand up for their own beliefs and the confidence to allow others to challenge them. They are selfless in their pursuit of the success of and for others. Leadership will never be a success if the aim is self-promotion or glory.

I believe that it is healthy to remember that your leadership is temporary and that you are just the author of one chapter in a school's history, a custodian; your aim must be to ensure that it is a great chapter and actually so good that it sets up the next one to be even better and creates a legacy...

10
Legacy

'*What you leave behind is not what is engraved in stone monuments, but what is woven into the lives of others.*'

Pericles

Like many educators, I have occasionally come across former students or their parents, who have been keen to tell me about their lives since leaving my class or school. It is sobering and humbling when someone you may remember as a shy, boisterous or friendly ten-year-old taps you on the shoulder with a 'Hello, sir. Do you remember me?' and as you turn to face a fully grown woman or man, sometimes with their own young family in tow, recognition dawns. They tell you with pride about their careers, their experiences, their lives. You listen with a swell of joy and of accomplishment, as you remember the time they spoke on a stage for the first time in a play or concert, having been the quiet, nervous kid at the start of the year, sat in the shadows. You might even shed a tear as they talk about becoming a teacher themselves. What you know as you listen is that you, in some small way, had a role to play: that the sense of purpose that led you to the classroom has been of benefit to another human being. As you stand there, reminiscing, you know that, for all the trials and challenges you faced in your career, there before you is a tangible example of legacy.

In this final chapter, I want to take a little time to reflect on that sense of purpose and to share the idea of legacy that I hope drives us all just a little bit and that has certainly been my motivation for writing this book. It is, after all, a sense of purpose that pushes us through the toughest and most challenging of times and helps us to get out of bed every morning to meet the task and responsibility of helping to educate every student, every day.

In the summer of 2018 I was invited to speak at an event in Madrid run by the Advanced Leadership Foundation. The core focus was on how we prepare the next generation to lead us through the challenges of the future. At the event I had the unbelievable honour of meeting with and listening to the 44th President of the United States of America, Barack Obama. His challenge to us was clear.

He told us that, 'Rapid changes across the globe had put massive strains on our social and political institutions.' He went on to explain that one of the key reasons for the rise in nationalism, in so many countries, was partly symptomatic of that change and had led to people becoming increasingly fearful of one another. He used this context to explain why he and his wife were now so committed to the future of young people and to the nurturing of the next generation of leaders. 'It is important,' he said, 'to focus on education, climate change, how to grow an economy and how to provide greater social equity and cohesion for example.' He explained that, 'In all of these issues, we are going to have to train our young people to think differently, to adapt to these new circumstances and to promote a new generation of leaders.'

He continued by saying, 'One of the things I learned as President of the United States is that most problems are not technical; most of the problems are human by nature; they have to do with politics, greed and jealousy, conflict and tribalism. They are all the things that keep us separated and prevent us from thinking together.' He clarified that the challenge therefore was, 'to encourage young people to think differently about problems and to form new kinds of institutions and ways of organising our societies'.

In his view, real change in education is necessary because, 'The way we organised education was to take people from farms into factories and office buildings, so we taught them to sit still and do repetitive tasks over and over again. We separated out the higher functions of engineering or physics or brain work from the manual labour that was required. Now we are in a society where we want every young person to think differently, collaboratively; to learn how to solve problems and to be able to work in teams. That requires a new model of education.'

In my humble opinion, he should know. There are a number of issues he raised that, for me, form the foundations of the legacy that we need to build.

Firstly, how can we best ensure that our children are able to cope with the rapid changes across the world, part technological, environmental, societal and economic, changes that have led to people feeling displaced, vulnerable and angry?

People are desperate for leadership and for the authorities they elected to find answers. One of the great challenges we face as educators is to find ways to ensure that our children are less reliant on others than we are and maybe that means we have to find new ways to teach. I see our children as potentially the most independent generation ever; they are born in an age where they have more chances to be active citizens than ever before, as consumers, as social leaders and as participants in democracy. The #NeverAgain movement founded by the unbelievably courageous and determined teenage survivors of the tragic and horrific shootings at Marjory Stoneman Douglas High School in Parkland is testament to that.

In order to achieve that potential, however, young people need our support and guidance. They need to learn how to use the tools at their disposal with wisdom and with a deep sense of morality. We cannot ignore modern culture or technology, nor can we seek to have total control over it before we integrate it into the education process. Teachers must have the courage to let our kids free a little, to trust them more and to control them less. Otherwise we simply perpetuate that culture of dependency that has left so many people feeling helpless. Our very mental health relies on our ability to feel in control of the events and circumstances around us. We must do a better job of instilling in our young people that opportunity but also the responsibilities that freedom brings with it.

Whilst young children need routines and structure in order to feel secure, we do need to ask questions about how we prepare our children to be able to cope better with uncertainty, change and less predictable pathways through life, rather than promising them that if they do X, Y will definitely happen. As I discussed earlier in the book, maybe we need to challenge the idea that formal education is finite, ending at the age of 18 or 21; maybe we need to ensure that learning and the access to it is a lifetime commitment, where apprenticeships, university or other opportunities are open to all at any age, at any time and in flexible ways. We need to reconfigure the idea that education is a preparation for life so that the idea becomes one where education is a constant through life.

As well as exploring what and how we teach, we need to explore what the days, terms and years at school look like. Many of the structures we have currently are there for the benefit of staff and parents, but are they really focused on the best experiences for our kids? Days, weeks and timetables that are always the same simply can't help prepare our children appropriately for a world beyond factories and office buildings. No one said it would be easy but the easy and most efficient option is not going to ensure the success of our system, so that it is relevant to future generations. The world's great innovations and evolutions do not happen by doing the same thing more efficiently; efficiency really is not enough. Our future depends on different.

Obama's observation that, 'Most problems are not technical; most of the problems are human by nature; they have to do with politics, greed and jealousy, conflict and tribalism' is really challenging and is familiar not just in a wider societal context but in education itself. Remember Steve Wozniak, the co-founder of Apple, saying to me that, 'When we debate education, we spend too long arguing over what we teach, rather than what really matters, which is how we learn.' That underlines for me that together we need to focus on a number of things and change the way we work on them. Education, like life, cannot be simply structured or compartmentalised. We can't define schooling with a 'one-size-fits-all' model, with set outcomes that ensure a certain future.

We need to remember that education isn't neatly sequential; you don't start by teaching children how to do stuff and then teach them what to do with it and finally the human qualities needed for it to be successful. Education is about human development and therefore education must be holistic; skills, knowledge and behaviours must be contextualised and developed together.

There must be a more mature and objective recognition that so much of the frustrating inertia that has prevented real education transformation over the last

50 years or so has been caused not by technical challenges but actually because of 'politics, greed and jealousy, conflict and tribalism'. Whether it is the result of clashing political ideology, the destabilising nature of new governments constantly changing policy, the greed of people who have vested financial interests, like some publishers who will try to steer education for the benefit of their shareholders, or even the jealousy amongst various 'experts' caused by the anxiety of who is better known, more popular or getting more 'airtime' – none of this must be allowed to dominate the debate or to hamper real, constructive development and progress. We owe our children better than that and if we are to expect them to lead the world into a better place, then we need to be the role models of the right behaviour.

Perhaps Obama's most challenging reflection, however, is his observation as to why change in education and a new debate about it are vital. There is no doubt that mass education was created to ensure that people were trained for jobs and therefore to have a future, to take them from the fields to the factories in order to fan the flames of the industrial revolution and the economy that would come with it. Although for most of us, in most developed countries, that revolution was already coming to an end when we were born, we have been able to see it unfold in the Far East and especially in China – a country that so skilfully took the traditional educational models of our own industrial revolution and refined them to catalyse theirs. Interestingly, in China, they have been far faster to identify that their economic sustainability now lies beyond industry and depends on the next phase of the economic 'S' curve: innovation. As a result, they have started to explore radical reforms to reinvent their education model. In 2013, for example, the Chinese government produced a set of regulations called 'Ten regulations to lessen academic burden for primary school students' (Strauss, 2013), and they are:

1. **Transparent admissions:** Admission to a school cannot take into account any achievement certificates or examination results. Schools must admit all students based on their residency without considering any other factors.

2. **Balanced grouping:** Schools must place students into classes and assign teachers randomly. Schools are strictly forbidden to use any excuse to establish 'fast-track' and 'slow-track' classes.

3. **'Zero-starting-point' teaching:** All teaching should assume all first-grade students begin at zero proficiency. Schools should not artificially impose higher academic expectations and expedite the pace of teaching.

4. **No homework:** No written homework is allowed in primary schools. Schools can however assign appropriate experiential homework by working with parents and community resources to arrange field trips, library visits and craft activities.

5. **Reduced testing:** No standardised testing is allowed for grades 1 to 3; for 4th grade and up, standardised testing is only allowed once per semester for

Chinese language, maths, and foreign languages. Other types of tests cannot be given more than twice per semester.

6. **Categorical evaluation:** Schools can only assess students using the categories of 'Exceptional', 'Excellent', 'Adequate', and 'Inadequate', replacing the traditional 100-point system.

7. **Minimising supplemental materials:** Schools can use at most one type of material to supplement the textbook and must have parental consent. Schools and teachers are forbidden to recommend, suggest or promote any supplemental materials to students.

8. **Strictly forbidding extra classes:** Schools and teachers cannot organise or offer extra instruction after regular school hours or during winter and summer breaks and other holidays. Public schools and their teachers cannot organise or participate in extra instructional activities.

9. **Minimum of one hour of physical exercise:** Schools are to guarantee the offering of physical education classes in accordance with the national curriculum, physical activities and eye exercise during recess.

10. **Strengthening enforcement:** Education authorities at all levels of government shall conduct regular inspection and monitoring of actions to lessen students' academic burden and publish findings. Individuals responsible for academic burden reduction are held accountable by the government.

For any country, but particularly one as focused on tradition and industrialisation as China, this is extraordinary. We cannot get left behind these radical changes in education and therefore need to recognise and act upon Obama's challenge. We need to ensure that our education system is focused on wanting 'Every young person to think differently, collaboratively; to learn how to solve problems and to be able to work in teams…'

Perhaps we have spent too long on the idea that we must sift our children and sort them into categories that fit certain roles and jobs. We need to realise that segregation and a system predicated on competition simply isn't relevant now.

Gareth Southgate led the England football team to their most successful World Cup performance in over 50 years in Russia in 2018, by recognising that he needed to diversify his coaching team, bringing in experts from different sports and specialisms, in order to find new, innovative ways forward – something that Sir Clive Woodward had done with the England World Cup-winning rugby union team in 2003. Gareth, like Clive, broke the cycle of doing the same thing in order to find the answer by challenging himself and his team to collaborate in new ways and, by so doing, to think differently.

Collaboration, and a commitment to it, is the future not only for education but for society, and we must do much, much more to connect through what we have in common rather than polarise through what drives us apart.

Society needs diversity; it always has and always will. We need to appreciate, though, that people have a right to move from one thing to another so that they can seize opportunities, realise dreams and adapt to the landscape of their lives more easily.

In Chapter 2, I referred to the 2013 OECD report 'Skills Outlook', which explored four key challenges for us to consider as we develop education policy for the future. It highlighted that firstly there was a concern that certain countries and states were overly reliant on the acquisition of formal qualifications rather than the development of actual skills in their school systems and that, as a result, young people in those countries would find it increasingly difficult to compete for work in the global market. It does appear that whilst academic and technical education is hugely important, it has increasingly squeezed out the crucial human development, holistic improvement and opportunities children need. We need to ensure that we still allow young people to enjoy school for the experience itself, for the sheer joy of discovering and exploring new concepts, skills and knowledge: cultural, scientific and intellectual. None of that can be accomplished if the core focus is to compete in some false 'arms race' for positions in global test rankings. As we think of our legacy we need to take heed of Eric Hoffer's (2010) warning in his book, *The True Believer*: 'In times of change learners inherit the earth, while the learned find themselves beautifully equipped to deal with a world that no longer exists.'

The second key finding of the OECD report was that interpersonal skills were now considered of far more importance than routine cognition, something Obama touched on when he talked of teaching 'them to sit still and do repetitive tasks over and over again'. We must introduce a new narrative to the conversations about the future of education that takes into account not only where we are but where we are going and, to that end, we need to find ways to stop developing policy and strategy based on the past or even the present, but instead heavily focus on the future. Far too much of what happens in education is reactive. We don't want future generations to maintain the world the way it is; we want them to change it for the better and that means we need to help them to think contrarily, to challenge, to question and to promote a dynamic restlessness that comes from curiosity.

Above all things, we need to make that a central tenant of our legacy. We must commit to nurturing the curiosity of young children, so that it becomes a lifelong trait. The world isn't standing still, nor must we. Humankind has evolved because of its constant desire to learn.

The third OECD finding was an extension of that thought and underlines the need for young people to be able to learn, adapt and change throughout their lives – something I believe we saw the importance of during the global financial crisis of 2007/08, when many well-educated people around the world, with good, stable jobs, found themselves in real trouble. People who had done what was asked of them and who had built a world of stability for themselves and their families felt cut adrift, unable to take control. The world is no longer about building walls to protect us; it is about filling backpacks to help us on our ongoing journey.

Legacy is an interesting concept, especially for a teacher; for many of us, we never see what happens in the long term for our students. As a primary school teacher, the young people I taught left at 11 years old and remained frozen in time in my head, but every so often, I would hear stories about where they had gone and what they had done. Occasionally, I see pictures of them on social media with families of their own, with careers and lives carved out of their childhood experiences. You also, occasionally, hear about the young people who left your school and found tragedy, disappointment or failure. We cannot control our children's futures and we shouldn't seek to, but we do contribute to the chances they will have and the tools they'll need in order to make the most of them. Our impact in the long term may be abstract but we must have faith in its long-term importance.

I often say to teachers and school leaders that they may never see the full effect of their decisions but they must trust that their impact will be felt. It is for that reason that we need to remember that our core focus cannot be on grades and end-of-year outcomes; it needs to be on something much bigger – the longer game. We may only touch a young person's life for a brief moment in time, but we must ensure that we contribute to a far longer journey.

If as educators we want to have an impact on the future then we need to have an idea of what we want that future to be, and as I come to the last part of this book, I want to share my own, personal aspiration for what I hope we can all contribute to. All human beings want to be of value; all human beings want to believe that they can lead lives where they have choices and some control. Some human beings realise early the power and potential of a life lived and of purpose, whilst some realise late and some… too late.

For society to thrive, to reconnect and to be better, we need people to reconnect with each other and most importantly with themselves. People need to feel valued and of value; they need to know that they have a purpose. We know that in many ways, a growing number of people feel undervalued and some helpless. The growing issues around mental health and the anger and resentment showing itself in society, through the increasing polarisation and the resurgence in extremism that Obama alluded to, benefit no one but do serve to destabilise and disrupt both the individual and society.

Educators are, like it or not, some of the most important people in changing the future. It has to be our aim to help to bring the best of our society together: the people and the organisations that best exemplify and champion the role of active citizenship, of values and of purpose, people and organisations who believe and evidence that we, you and I, can change the world for the better. School should be that gathering point, the foundation stone of learning and of collaboration on which ideas, philosophies and the future are built. It takes a village…

This is not meant to be a grandiose vision but a granular one; it is Gandhi's 'Be the change you want to see.'

I believe that our wider legacy should be to help to create a simple catalyst for what I see as the five core themes of a life, themes I highlighted in the book's introduction:

- to be healthy
- to be skilled
- to be aware
- to be hopeful
- to be of value.

We need to explore how as schools we can play our role in supporting the five phases of life, both as an organisation and as a collaborative partner. We need to influence:

- **Emergence:** Before birth, we must support young families so that they can create nurturing environments that best prepare and provide for children in the first phases of life, to help to make the early links between the five core themes.
- **Education:** We must focus on how we use formal education to ensure that our emerging young citizens are prepared for the world they are going to inherit, that their knowledge, skills, attributes and behaviours empower them and inspire them to head confidently into the next phase of life.
- **Activism:** As organisations, educators, employers and institutions, we must work together to ensure that our young people feel that they have a place and a purpose as emerging adult citizens in society, so that they feel that they have the opportunity to make their mark. Moving on, we must consider how we help them understand the growing of their responsibility as they move on to phase four.
- **Leadership:** How do we ensure that the gained experience, vision and actions of their activism are not wasted and are utilised in order to take on leadership and responsibility for developing the phases further and for evolving the narratives and sense of empowerment for the next generation?
- **Legacy:** How do we ensure that our elders continue to thrive, to be supported and most importantly to feel valued? How do we capture and use their wisdom to inform and educate future cohorts?

We know that our world today is a more complex place than it has ever been; the exponential changes driven by the digital revolution, together with the extra-ordinary, and at times frightening, opportunities that those changes herald, mean, maybe, that for the first time in human history, we no longer feel in control of our own destiny. The damage that we have done to our own planet's ecosystem demands that we live our lives differently. The economic imbalance that leads to a growing sense of inequality and opportunity in what should be a more open world means that our children have some daunting issues to solve, if we and our planet are to have any legacy at all… but I am optimistic.

Over the last few years I have met thousands of educators around the globe, young and old – people who care passionately about their students and the future they can create. I also believe that the current generation of young people emerging through our education system could be the greatest generation in our history. There are more children accessing education than ever before; it is a job far from finished but at least we are increasing our global talent pool.

Human resource is without doubt the most precious natural resource of all right now, because it is only our species that can solve the problems that we have largely created. To do that we need to unearth and nurture the very best of us, wherever they may be. More than ever before, we must realise and respect that talent won't just be found in the academically gifted or privileged, but in a multitude of skills and abilities. We must cast our net far and wide, broaden our horizons and recalibrate what formal education is seeking to achieve.

The time for false wars and debates must now be over and so I end where I began: with a call for peace and collaboration. I urge us all to seek out our common goals and beliefs to find ways to use education as a means to define a better, brighter future for our children, grandchildren and the generations beyond.

The truth is that we may never see the outcomes of the changes we begin today but we will be remembered for being the generation that catalysed them. Let us be the role models who inspire our children to believe that they can lead a better, safer world, a world where all of our human traits are used to their full potential.

As Aristotle was reported to have remarked, 'We are rational animals pursuing knowledge for its own sake. We live by art and reasoning.'

We are born naturally and selflessly collaborative; other close relatives, like chimpanzees, collaborate but only if there is something in it for them; young children enjoy helping others for the act itself. As people we are naturally empathetic; we understand what others think based upon our knowledge of the world. We tell stories, we dream, we imagine things about ourselves and others, and we spend a great deal of time thinking about the future and analysing the past. We are able to accumulate wisdom and knowledge through our collaborative approach to development. We also have the capacity to do evil; whilst we are not the only species to be tribal, to fight wars or to kill, our intelligence means that we can do so on a huge scale and for simply emotional and ideological differences.

I do not believe for one minute that teachers have total or even primary responsibility for the future but we can and should certainly be of substantive influence; the vast majority of people who have changed the world, for better or for worse, have been to school; they have sat in a classroom much like ours today, experiencing teaching, learning and social interactions just as our students are now. Our children spend more waking hours in our company than they do in anyone else's, and that means we have to own our share of the future. Queen Rania of Jordan said at an address to the World Economic Forum in May 2013, 'Good teachers teach, great teachers transform.'

I recently interviewed Barry Barish, the 2017 Nobel Prize-winning physicist; he is a genuine genius, the world's leading expert on gravitational waves. We talked a great deal about education and the future. During our conversation, he talked at length about what he looked for in the people who joined his team at CalTech (California Institute of Technology). For him, the most important characteristic of someone searching for answers or pathways to the future is curiosity. Therefore he is not so bothered about what people know, but whether they can ask questions… relentlessly. Maybe this is the best legacy we should hope for: that as educators, we nurture curiosity, that we help our children develop knowledge and experiences in such a way that it ensures that they are always able to ask questions, that they realise that learning is not finite and not for tests and exams, but that it is fuel for always being able to know more and to be more. We are a unique species and within that species we are all individually distinctive.

Education can only provide a journey to the future if we don't try to cling on to the ghosts of the past. Tomorrow is yet to be written and, in the most traditional sense, we need to provide the pen and ink but not the story.

As I finish, I hope that for those of you who have made your way through with me, you will generate your own ideas, debates and collaborations catalysed by my simple thoughts; that you have the confidence and belief that as an educator or someone involved in the lives of young people, you are special; and that the responsibilities you bear can be turned into a legacy for which society will eternally be thankful.

Go forward, good luck; change the world.

Bibliography

BlueEQ™ (2017), 'Emotional intelligence and Google's Aristotle Project', https://blueeq.com/wp-content/uploads/2017/02/BlueEQ-Emotional-Intelligence-and-Google.pdf

Canfield, J., Hansen, M.V. and Newmark, A. (2013), *The Original Chicken Soup for the Soul: 20th Anniversary Edition*. Cos Cob, CT: Chicken Soup for the Soul Publishing.

Clinton, W. J. (2000), *Public Papers of the Presidents of the United States 2000: Book 1: William J. Clinton: January 1 to June 26, 2000*. Washington, DC: Office of the Federal Register.

Center for Information and Research on Civic Learning and Engagement (2016), 'Donald Trump and young voters', https://civicyouth.org/wp-content/uploads/2016/06/Trump-and-Youth-Vote.pdf

Committee on Higher Education (1963), 'The Robbins Report'. London: Her Majesty's Stationery Office, http://www.educationengland.org.uk/documents/robbins/robbins1963.html

Dolton, P., Marcenaro, O., de Vries, R. and She, P.-W. (2018), 'Global teacher status index 2018', Varkey Foundation, https://www.varkeyfoundation.org/media/4867/gts-index-13-11-2018.pdf

Drucker, P. T. (1992), *Managing for the Future: The 1990s and Beyond*. New York, NY: Penguin.

Drucker, P. F. (2008), *Managing Oneself*. Boston, MA: Harvard Business Review.

Frammolino, R. and Boucher, G. (2001), 'Rap was Eminem's roots and road out of poverty', 21 February, *LA Times*, http://articles.latimes.com/2001/feb/21/news/mn-28235/2

Gallo, C. (2010), *The Innovation Secrets of Steve Jobs*. New York, NY: McGraw Hill.

Gerver, R. (2013), *Change: Learn to Love It, Learn to Lead It*. London: Portfolio Penguin.

Gerver, R. (2016), 'Finding a sense of higher purpose', *TEDx Talk*, www.youtube.com/watch?v=0qYTf9evWeY

Hirsch, E. D. (1988), *Cultural Literacy: What Every American Needs to Know*. New York, NY: Vintage Books.

HM Queen Elizabeth II (2010), 'Address to the United Nations General Assembly', 6 July, https://www.royal.uk/address-united-nations-general-assembly-6-july-2010

Hoffer, E. (2010), *The True Believer: Thoughts on the Nature of Mass Movements* (2nd edn.). New York, NY: Harper Collins.

Ipsos MORI (2005), 'How Britain voted in 2005', https://www.ipsos.com/ipsos-mori/en-uk/how-britain-voted-2005

Ipsos MORI (2017a), 'Veracity Index 2017', https://www.ipsos.com/sites/default/files/ct/news/documents/2017-11/trust-in-professions-veracity-index-2017-slides.pdf

Ipsos MORI (2017b), 'How Britain voted in the 2017 election', https://www.ipsos.com/ipsos-mori/en-uk/how-britain-voted-2017-election

Isaacson, W. (2015), *Steve Jobs: The Exclusive Biography*. London: Abacus.

Kennedy, J. F. (1963), 'Remarks prepared for delivery at the Trade Mart in Dallas, TX', 22 November, undelivered, https://www.jfklibrary.org/Research/Research-Aids/JFK-Speeches/Dallas-TX-Trade-Mart-Undelivered_19631122.aspx

Keyes, M. (2017), *The Break*. London: Penguin.

King, M. L. (1963), *Strength to Love*. New York, NY: Collins-World.

Lash, J. P. (1997), *Helen and Teacher: Story of Helen Keller and Anne Sullivan Macy* (revised edn.). London: Da Capo Press.

Lehrer, J. (2011), 'The Steve Jobs approach to teamwork', *Wired*, https://www.wired.com/2011/10/the-steve-jobs-approach-to-teamwork/

Mandela, N. (2003), 'Lighting your way to a better future', 16 July, University of the Witwatersrand, Johannesburg, http://db.nelsonmandela.org/speeches/pub_view.asp?pg=item&ItemID=NMS909&txtstr=education%20is%20the%20most%20powerful

Maslow, A. H. (1966), *The Psychology of Science: A Reconnaissance*. New York, NY: Harper and Row.

Morrison, M. (2012), 'Google's Project Oxygen – 8 point plan to help managers improve', *RapidBi*, https://rapidbi.com/google-project-oxygen-8-point-plan-to-help-managers/

OECD (2013), 'OECD Skills Outlook 2013', https://www.oecd.org/skills/piaac/Skills%20volume%201%20(eng)--full%20v12--eBook%20(04%2011%2013).pdf

Oxford Dictionary of English (2010), 'knowledge'. Oxford: Oxford University Press.

Oxford Dictionary of English (2010), 'skill'. Oxford: Oxford University Press.

Pouliot, C. and Godbout, J. (2014), 'Thinking outside the "knowledge deficit" box', *EMBO Reports*, 15, (8), 833–35.

Short, J. F., Hughes, L. A. and Dooley, B. D. (2006), *Studying Youth Gangs*. Lanham, MD: Rowman and Littlefield.

Standing, E. M. (1998), *Maria Montessori: Her Life and Work*. New York, NY: Penguin Putnam Inc.

Strauss, V. (2013), 'China's 10 new and surprising school reform rules', 30 October, *The Washington Post*, https://www.washingtonpost.com/people/valerie-strauss/

Viña, G. (2016), 'Young graduates struggle to find skilled work', *Financial Times*, https://www.ft.com/content/480d0ad6-0ba9-11e6-b0f1-61f222853ff3

Woodward, E., Surdek, S. and Ganis, M. (2010), *A Practical Guide to Distributed Scrum*. Boston, MA: IBM Press.

World Economic Forum (2013), 'Top ten quotes of Davos 2013', https://www.weforum.org/agenda/2013/01/top-ten-quotes-of-davos-2013/

World Economic Forum (2018), 'The future of education, according to experts at Davos', https://www.weforum.org/agenda/2018/01/top-quotes-from-davos-on-the-future-of-education/

Wright, W. (1900), *Letter to Octave Chanute*, 13 May, https://en.wikiquote.org/wiki/Wilbur_Wright

Yousafzai, M. (2017), 'To every child...', 20 November, 6:12am (Tweet), https://twitter.com/malala/status/932612718825299969

Index